'Educational Leadership for Social Justice' series

Tony Bush and David Middlewood, *Leading and Managing People in Education* (2005)

Jacky Lumby with Marianne Coleman, *Leadership and Diversity* (2007)

Tony Bush, *Leadership and Management Development in Education* (2008)

Leading and Managing Extended Schools

Ensuring Every Child Matters

David Middlewood and
Richard Parker

⑨SAGE

Los Angeles • London • New Delhi • Singapore • Washington DC

SAGE Publications Limited
1 Oliver's Yard
55 City Road
London EC1Y 1SP

SAGE Publications Inc
2455 Teller Road
Thousand Oaks, California 91320

SAGE Publications India Pvt Ltd
B1/I1 Mohan Cooperative Industrial Area
Mathura Road
New Delhi-110 044

SAGE Publications Asia-Pacific Pte Ltd
33 Pekin Street #02–01
Far East Square
Singapore 048763

Library of Congress Control Number: 2008931997

British Library Cataloguing in Publication data

A catalogue record for this book is available from the British
Library

ISBN: 978-1-4129-4829-6
ISBN: 978-1-4129-4830-2 (pbk)

Typeset by Dorwyn, Wells, Somerset
Printed in Great Britain by CPI Antony Rowe,
Chippenham, Wiltshire
Printed on paper from sustainable resources

Mixed Sources
Product group from well-managed
forests and other controlled sources
www.fsc.org Cert no. SGS-COC-2953
© 1996 Forest Stewardship Council
FSC

Contents

Notes on the authors

David Middlewood is a Research Fellow in the Institute of Education at the University of Warwick, and he previously worked for the universities of Lincoln and Leicester, where he was Deputy Director of the Centre for Educational Leadership and Management. Prior to this, David had a successful career in schools and colleges, including nine years as headteacher of an 11–18 comprehensive school. He has published widely on strategic management, practitioner research, curriculum management and especially on human resources. David has been a visiting professor in New Zealand and South Africa and has been involved in research on a range of topics including inclusive schools, associate staff, leadership teams and succession planning.

Richard Parker is Principal of Beauchamp College, a large multicultural community college in Leicestershire. Prior to that, for ten years, Richard was headteacher of Lodge Park Technology College in Corby, one of the first specialist technology colleges in the country. During his career, he has been a research associate at the National College of School Leadership, a member of the Specialist Schools and Academies Trust Council, an associate tutor with the University of Leicester and a founding member of a government think tank on school diversity. Richard's commitment to the extended services agenda has been influential in making Beauchamp a nationally recognized reference site for extended schools.

David and Richard have collaborated on various ventures, including being co-editors of the practitioner journal, *Headship Matters*, from 1999 to 2005. Together with Jackie Beere, they produced *Creating a Learning School*, published by Paul Chapman Publishing/Sage in 2005.

Series Editor's Foreword

While politicians in most countries regularly stress the importance of education in national development, and similarly note the evolving nature of modern societies as they become more diverse and complex, actual government legislation usually deals with these issues quite separately. In fact, of course, as previous books in this series have shown, the same people are dealing with these same issues all the time. Education does not exist in some kind of vacuum, separate from the many and diverse influences which impact upon the child, young person and the adult.

For sustainable social change and greater social justice to occur, the key is surely to begin with the early stages of life where possible, while addressing current needs wherever they demand attention. Community Schooling in various countries has in the past attempted to address this, but in the United States and the United Kingdom, specific legislation has begun to place a focus on the child at the centre of societal and community development, with the understanding that in itself this will address issues of much wider significance.

As Glover and Harris (2007) pointed out in their extensive literature review of the UK's Every Child Matters (ECM) and Extended Schools, most of the literature took the form of evaluation reports and media articles, with very few academic journals and no mainstream texts. This book in this series is therefore extremely timely, fulfilling a need in one of the most significant areas of educational development.

Educational leadership and management now readily acknowledges its role in this wider context and stresses its concern with social justice, diversity, morality and spirituality. All these concerns and high level skills in leadership are required if those intended to benefit from ECM and extended schooling are to do so.

The authors of this book, one a former headteacher and now a university research fellow, and one a principal of a large full-service extended school in England, have seen many examples of the ways in which schools, children's centres, and other establishments are fulfilling their obligations in this field but going that 'extra mile' and offering exciting and often inspiring services which are leading in some cases to community regeneration. Whether leaders in any of these organizations are at the beginning, a little way along the path, or already well established, they will all – as well as academic and professional practitioners and researchers – find food for thought, inspiration and not least suggestions for developing their practice in their workplace and local community. It is in this way that the greater issues in societies and nations will begin to be addressed in a form which will have lasting impact.

David Middlewood
Series Editor

Preface

This series of books is concerned with how leadership in education can contribute to social change which brings greater social justice. This cannot be achieved unless it addresses some of the major issues in communities, such as inequalities in opportunities for employment, economic prosperity, health and general well-being. Both in the United States' 'No Child Left Behind' and in the United Kingdom's 'Every Child Matters', national governments have signalled intentions to do this, and in doing so, have placed the child – and therefore schools – at the centre of the attempted solutions to all of these issues. While both these countries, and indeed several others, have previously attempted what is generally called community education, these recent initiatives are different in the emphasis they put on the integration of education with other services such as health and social welfare.

In being excited by the extended school initiative in the UK, we are both well aware that good schools everywhere have always offered after-hours activities, clubs and facilities, contributing to what has been known as the 'hidden curriculum'. However, in extended and full-service schools, these things are not just a valuable optional extra; they are integral to the local community's understanding of what a school is and what it provides. Through facilities such as Sure Start, Children's Centres, Neighbourhood Centres, as well as provision for senior citizens, lifelong learning becomes not just a pleasant possibility for those motivated to learn in the conventional sense, but something which addresses the core needs and aspirations of many families.

Drawing on the inspiration of a few examples of schools which appeared to be making a significant difference, we set out to explore ways in which leaders and managers of extended and full-service schools are already helping – or planning – to transform communities. We discovered that, in doing so, these leaders had found the very nature of their schools had changed and continued to change – in staffing, structures, resourcing and inevitably in leadership and management. Of course, there is a long way to go and much more to do, but we believe that even those who are only at the beginning of their journey to becoming an extended school will find inspiration and, we hope, practical help in this book.

Firstly, in the book, we set the scene and explore the ideas in extended schooling, examining its impact on school features and on leadership. We then describe the implications for staffing, accountability, parents and the many new partnerships which develop out of this new kind of schooling. Resourcing is also explored and we have tried to suggest some ideas for readers' reflections in terms of possible actions to be taken. Case examples are widely used and we have drawn fully on discussions with social workers, health workers and community helpers as much as educationalists in offering these. Throughout, we have been reminded that the individual child/pupil/student remains central to all developments and that the 'day job' of the leaders is to keep that constantly in focus. The goal of achieving social justice, while at the same time reducing the underperformance of some schools, is likely to continue to prove difficult, but the signs of the impact of extended schooling on this are encouraging.

The schools we visited or contacted included nursery, primary, secondary and special and, since schools appear to use different terms for their learners, we have adopted the use of 'pupils' for children of primary education age and 'students' for secondary education age throughout the book.

We would not have been able to complete this project without the generosity (especially with their time) and cooperation of the many people with whom we have met and discussed their experiences and ideas. Some of these people were happy for us to use their and their schools' actual names, whilst others preferred more anonymity. We have respected their wishes in all cases. In addition, two people from Beauchamp College have been invaluable in enabling us to write this book. Kanta Chauhan has been a tower of strength with her patience, commitment and technical prowess; Bob Mitchell has been a huge help with the sharing of his knowledge, contacts and experience, especially in the field of partnerships.

We wish to thank Marianne Lagrange and Matthew Waters at Sage Publications for their support. David owes thanks to Janine, Tim, John, Tracey, Paul, Sam and Michael for keeping him constantly inspired in adult learning and, above all, to Jacqui for her unwavering faith in him, and Richard thanks Nora for her encouragement, her support and her belief.

David Middlewood
Richard Parker

Glossary

AOT	Adult Other Than Teacher
ASPECT	Association of Professionals in Education and Children's Trust
ATL	Association of Teachers and Lecturers
CABMAG	Comberton and Bassingbourn, Melbourn and Gamlingay
CAF	Common Assessment Framework
CAMHS	Child and Adolescent Mental Health Services
CEO	Chief Executive Officer
DCSF	Department for Children, Schools and Families
DfES	Department for Education and Skills
ECM	Every Child Matters
ETC	Extending to Communities
FSES	Full-Service Extended School
ICT	Information Communications Technology
LA	Local Authority
LOOSH	Learning Out Of School Hours
NAHT	National Association of Head Teachers
NCLB	No Child Left Behind
NCSL	National College of School Leadership
NPQICL	National Professional Qualification in Integrated Centre Leadership
NUT	National Union of Teachers
OECD	Organization for Economic and Social Development
OFSTED	Office for Standards in Education
PCT	Primary Care Trust
PEP	Personal Education Plan
PTA	Parent Teacher Association
PTFA	Parent, Teacher and Friends Association
SBM	Site Based Management
SEN	Special Educational Needs
SENCO	Special Educational Needs Coordinator

TDA	Teacher Development Agency
TES	*Times Education Supplement*
UNESCO	United Nations Educational, Scientific and Cultural Organization
UNICEF	United Nations International Children's Emergency Fund
YOT	Youth Offending Team

Part 1
The Concept and Context of Extended Schools

Introduction

For those with the view that there is nothing new in education or indeed in politics, the notion of schools being integral to their communities seems ironic. State schools in England and Wales, for example, were specifically designed in the nineteenth century to meet the basic needs of local communities, and only the wealthy or aspiring sent their sons away to private schools for a 'proper' (i.e. academic) education. Apart from some Boards of Governors, the actual people of the communities were not involved in school, except for ensuring their children attended school and were later supported in terms of homework, school functions and fund-raising. In researching for this book, and talking with men and women who had been secondary school pupils in the 1950s, a common image is of them looking over the fences in school holidays at school playgrounds and playing fields which lay deserted, while they played games or kicked footballs in the streets. 'They were sacrosanct' said one man, 'and it never occurred to us to question the situation of waste.'

When the possibilities of extended and full-service provision schools are considered, and the ideas of 'open all hours', staggered hours of learning and part-time attendance changing the very nature of a school are reflected upon, there can be a realization that the extended school really has the potential to represent the biggest change in education for more than a century, as some of its exponents claim. In this first section, Chapter 1 examines the need for this change and how it has gathered impetus. Chapter 2 discusses some of the huge implications these changes have for those working in schools and living and working in their communities. Chapter 3 addresses the impact these same changes have upon our notions of what leadership in education involves, both conceptually and practically.

1

What are extended schools and why are they needed?

This chapter considers the following questions:

- What is meant by extended schools and how did they develop?
- What other educational developments link with it?
- What are the indicators of effective extended schools?

While extravagant claims have been made for various educational reforms as being the most important, none can have been as far-reaching as that for the development of extended schools, because its ultimate aim must be not to transform schools, or even education, but to *transform communities*. As West-Burnham (2006, p. 103) suggests:

> Pivotal to the long-term development of extended schools is the notion of community-moving from schools in a community through community schools to communities which include schools as part of their educational provision. There is a very important symbolic and semantic point ... when we will stop talking about extending schools and start talking about developing the community.

In one sense, this concept is revolutionary; in another, it is entirely logical, since what is the purpose of education if it is not to change, develop and improve the world in which we live? It is only revolutionary in terms of how we have come to perceive schools, as institutions separate from communities, with a specific purpose of preparing children and young people for adult life – especially through the gaining of qualifications.

From separation to community awareness

In the UK, despite the pioneering efforts of Henry Morris in the 1920s with the Cambridgeshire Village College, and the building of Community Colleges in the 1960s, the widespread model was of schools separated from their local environment, except for the provision of formal Adult Education Classes. Tim Brighouse, in a speech in the 1970s, described the typical purpose-built community college as a castle, neatly situated *outside* the population centres and 'surrounded by a lovely green moat'. Clearly, the drawbridge could be drawn up if the community needed to be kept out!

It is interesting to note that earlier efforts in both the USA and the UK were more successful in rural contexts – Barnard's and Dewey's ideas of the school as an embodiment of a democratic community in the USA were perhaps more easily realized there than in the growing turbulence of modern urban life.

In this urban context, the Children's Aid Society (founded in 1853) was involved in the USA's first compulsory education laws, and was eventually responsible for the creation of New York's first vocational schools and first free kindergartens. Until the 1980s however, the Society remained focused on health services and the integration of these with schools did not emerge until the programme for community schools got under way in New York. In both the USA and the UK, schools were for teaching and not much else.

This perception of schools as separate educational providers was gradually accompanied in several developed countries by a narrowness of focus as to the purpose of schooling, with a massive emphasis on testing and examination results, shown most powerfully perhaps in England and Wales. This performance culture (for an overview, see Gleeson and Husbands, 2001) was accentuated by the marketization of education and competition between schools. While parental involvement in their children's education was increasingly acknowledged as important, it was usually seen in terms of parental support for schools, rather than in terms of any kind of partnership for learning.

By the late 1990s however, Fullan (1998, p. 2), using an image similar to Brighouse's, could describe the fences of the school in several countries as 'tumbling down metaphorically speaking … as government policy, parent and community demands, corporate interests and ubiquitous technology have all scaled the walls of the school'.

Fullan was describing developments in school reform in countries such as Australia, Canada, the United States and the United Kingdom. In the last two countries in particular, there were a number of factors which made policy-makers, educationalists, public-service leaders and managers come to realize the dangers and impracticalities of schools operating in comparative isolation. These factors include:

1 A clear recognition that education alone could not be some kind of panacea for all of society's problems. In an increasingly globalized and competitive economy, the drive for a well-educated workforce as the key to economic success remained – and still remains – a central purpose, in developing countries as much as if not more than in developed ones. However, deficiencies in educational systems, including those of the United States and the United Kingdom, for a significant cohort of the future adult population and workforce, prompted Mortimore (1997) and Lewin and Kelley (1997) to suggest that the success of education in being effective in changing society was dependent on the complementary inputs from a variety of other areas.

> The fact of the matter is that education is just one factor – albeit an important one – in an overall mélange of conditions that determines productivity and economic competitiveness as well as the levels of crime, public assistance, political participation, health and so on. Education has the potential for powerful impacts in each of these areas if the proper supportive conditions and inputs are present. (Lewin and Kelley, 1997, p. 250)

2 An accumulation of research which showed that a huge variety of factors influenced the way in which humans learned effectively. Only some of these factors were possible for schools to utilize. An awareness of how the brain works, different styles of learning and of teaching, multiple intelligences, emotional intelligence, learning personalities and technological developments are all examples of 'new' knowledge which effective schools, looking beyond test results and wanting to see learning as central (Middlewood et al., 2005), have been able to use to a greater or lesser extent to improve learning and attitudes towards education.

  However, diet (and health generally), inadequate parenting, endemic circumstances of poverty, unemployment, social attitudes such as racism, 'gang culture' in crime and drug contexts are all examples of factors which hugely influence learning but on which schools have only limited influence. This is partly because of the simple fact that, however good a school is, a person up to the age of 16 years spends only a small percentage of his or her life at that school.

3 The undeniable links between the significant proportion of the school population emerging from the system as failures and their later (sometimes simultaneous) susceptibility to an involvement in lives which include unemployment, poverty, poor health (even lower life expectancy) and crime. The emergence of an 'under class' of a disaffected and detached section of society seemed to exemplify the gaps between the so-called 'haves and have-nots' in industrialized wealthy nations. Access to the professions, for example, was

automatically denied for those disadvantaged because of their failure to gain relevant qualifications.

4 The pressure on public-service systems, including education, caused by increasingly pluralist, multi-ethnic societies, as immigration to Western nations on a large scale increased significantly.

5 An awareness in those nations that legislation alone concerning equal opportunities for people regardless of gender, race, disability, religion, sexual orientation and age – however well intentioned – was proving inadequate in an attempt to develop harmonious societies.

6 The economic realization that the enormous financial resources given to supporting those at a disadvantage were failing to repay society through helping them to overcome their deprivations. In changing economic circumstances, especially of an ageing population, the need to move the focus to preventative and away from remedial measures became imperative.

7 Lastly, but by no means least, a number of extremely high-profile cases (notably in England, the Victoria Climbié Inquiry) focused public attention. While shocking the public into the acknowledgement that such things actually occurred, they equally significantly pointed out the explicit failures of the public services to prevent or alleviate them. In particular, the failures in communication and cooperation between social services, law and order, education and health authorities were stark in their weak accountability and poor integration (Gelsthorpe, 2006). As the Judge at the Climbié Inquiry noted:

> We said that, after the Maria Caldwell case, it must never happen again. It clearly has. We cannot afford to let it occur ever again, without being aware that everything in our power was done to prevent it.

From community to integration

For all its value, community education as known was essentially of a reactive nature. Communities and services waited to be called for by the schools and colleges to provide what they had to offer. Education still appeared to be incapable of proactivity in its relationships with its communities.

In the United States, a series of initiatives in the early 1990s – of family resource centres, full-service schools, youth service centres, Bridges to Success, etc. – were attempting to offer 'school-based health, social service and academic enrichment programs' (Dryfoos et al., 2005), and Community Schools with strongly integrated services began in 1994 in New York City. Dryfoos et al. (2005) identified the five elements of that community education provision as:

- early intervention

- parental involvement
- after-school enrichment
- individual attention
- social capital.

In 2001, the US Act, 'No Child Left Behind' (NCLB), attempted to enshrine rights and access to fundamental provision for all children in legislation. (But see Chapter 10 for important differences between NCLB and ECM).

In Scotland, New Community Schools began in 1998 with similar aims and the final evaluation report (Sammons et al., 2003) stressed the effectiveness of their multi-agency approaches amongst other benefits, as well as identifying many issues as yet unresolved.

In England and Wales, the Government's Green Paper of 2003 paved the way for the two seminal documents, Every Child Matters (2004) and the Children Act (2004).

Every Child Matters (ECM)

The five envisaged outcomes for every child underpin everything that the provision of services for children should strive to achieve and would be assessed by:

- being healthy (physically, mentally, emotionally, sexually)
- being safe (from bullying and discrimination, from neglect, violence, etc.)
- enjoying and achieving (being 'stretched' at primary and secondary schools, supported by families)
- making positive contributions (developing enterprise, decision-making, supporting the community and the environment)
- having economic well-being (having continuing post-school education/training, decent homes, access to transport, reasonable income).

It is easy to relate these outcomes to the point made above about how far conventional schools, even effective ones, can impact on some and not on others. It is also clear that the fact that every *child* matters means of course that every *person* matters, as it is children who will be the future transformers of society.

One further important point is worth stressing here. Obvious though it may seem, the word 'Every' in ECM does include every child, regardless of background, socio-economic context, and therefore children from prosperous, even privileged, families are equally affected. Most of the political discourse and research has understandably focused on the need to improve the lot of children in deprived circumstances, reduce poverty and enhance future prospects. We must not forget however that children from contexts that may not have economic or employment problems are extremely vulnerable in other areas. For example, rates of suicide and depression in young people in highly developed countries such as Australia, China, Japan, the UK and the USA are alarmingly high (80 per cent of these are girls in both the UK and the USA, and 70 per cent in Australia) and the greatest proportion of these come from 'middle-class' families. Levine's research (2005) found that children from affluent homes were three times more likely to suffer from anxiety and depression during their teenage years in the USA. Ten per cent of 5–16 year olds in the UK were found to be suffering from emotional/behavioural problems, compared with between six and nine per cent of adults. In a typical secondary school of 1000 pupils, 50 are seriously depressed, 100 are suffering significant distress, 5 to 10 girls have an eating disorder and 10 to 20 pupils have obsessive compulsive disorders, according to Wilson (2008, p. 9).

A combining of research reports over the period 2002–2006 suggested that the five main reasons for this situation were:

- the pressure to perform well in examinations
- the constant pressure from families to be engaged in numerous activities that were seen as 'improving'
- a materialistic outlook that seems to value looks, wealth and clothes above happiness – 'chasing unattainable lifestyles' (Restemeuer, 2008)
- an embedded drink culture
- a fragmentation of family/support units.

The first two of these are most evident in families with no significant economic or employment problems. In this book, our research has encompassed extended schooling, not only in areas of extreme deprivation, but also in those of relative prosperity, and more than one school leader told us of the pressure that children from prosperous and 'upwardly striving' families were constantly under. They suggested that the right of these children to be happy and healthy was as great as anyone else's and reminded us, as stated above, that *every* child matters.

Whatever their background, Britain's children were identified in a UNICEF report of 2007 as 'the unhappiest in the world', and the growth of mental health problems in the broadest sense was described by the World Health Organization (Troedson, 2005) as a time bomb ticking for the civilized world.

The Children Act (2004) provided the legislative framework for the reform of children's services, and included the establishment of Children's Centres, the appointment of a Children's Commissioner and various proposals for the integration of children's services, including the appointment of a Director of Children's Services at Local Authority level. These statutory changes – phased in – provide the structure within which ECM outcomes may be achieved. The provision for 'Extended Schools' is included here.

Other indicators of integration

Since the Act and ECM, there has been an acceptance in the UK of the need to integrate services for children across the professional bodies concerned. For example:

- The National Association of Education Inspectors, Advisers and Consultants became the Association of Professionals in Education and Children's Trust (ASPECT).
- The National College for School Leadership in England – described by Bush (2008, p. 73) as 'probably the most significant global initiative for leadership development' – now offers a National Professional Qualification in Integrated Centre Leadership (NPQICL).
- Most Local Government Authorities have appointed a Director of Children's Services – some of these are from education backgrounds, while some are from social services.
- All children's service provisions are inspected by the same authority.

Recognition at the highest level in the UK that it was unhelpful to see education as a separate process came in July 2007 when the national government's 'Department for Education and Skills' was replaced by the 'Department for Children, Schools and Families' (DCSF). We now need to examine the notion of extended schools and what it involves.

The place of extended schools

Given the aims of transforming community and the integration of those responsible for health, law and order and social welfare, it is worth reminding ourselves that we are concerned in this book with schools and the leadership and management of schools. It therefore needs to be acknowledged that schools are pivotal in everything described and discussed so far in this chapter. Dryfoos, one of the most important people in the United States's development of integrated services, was a researcher in adolescent behaviour, but she was clear that all coordinated support programmes 'had to be connected to the most influential institution in our society, public (i.e. state) schools' (Dryfoos et al., 2005, p. 9). Wilkins (2005, p. 30), in defining schooling as the technology which socializes children in ways which lead them to develop a long-term desire for learning, suggests that schools 'stand at the meeting point of politics, scholarship and community'.

Schools then are central to communities; two obvious facts underpin this:

- it is statutory for children to attend school and
- children spend vastly more time at school than they are likely to in medical centres, social care, etc. (with a few exceptions).

Prior to the formal establishment of extended schooling – and community schooling in, for example, the USA and Scotland – there had been various issues in education, and in society in these countries and several other Western nations, which impacted on schools in ways which complemented for effective schools their readiness for what extended schooling was to involve. These emerging issues, some specific to education, some in society at large, were inextricably linked with extended schooling, in that proposals for this initiative were natural developments from these issues, so that no extended or full-service school could be effective without consideration of them. Some of these are now briefly considered.

Diversity

As societies become increasingly pluralist, the focus has moved forward from ensuring equal opportunities by addressing inequities in access to achievement, status, etc. There is a recognition that the strength of a society or organization lies in its ability to acknowledge and utilize capability wherever it exists. 'Equity in difference' is a phrase widely used to describe this. Thus in education, a school staff which is at least as diverse as the community it reflects will have the strengths of a whole range of capabilities, probably drawing on the variety of these that exist in different ethnic cultures. Bush and Middlewood (2005, p. 96) suggest that, allowing for stereotyping, the potential for utilizing the strengths of, for example:

- a Japanese group ethic
- a Chinese work ethic
- African collaborative approaches
- Western problem-solving activities

is considerable, as well as of course the particular strengths associated with both males and females.

Inclusion

Closely related to diversity is the notion of inclusion, that is the right of all citizens to be included in society's or an organization's provisions and activities through a consideration of what people *can* do and not be prevented from so doing because of what they *cannot* do. Originally, in education in particular, this emphasis was especially on disability, those designated as having Special Educational Needs (SEN). The pressure to ensure SEN children were not missing out on opportunities by not being included in mainstream schools led to the closure of large numbers of special schools in England and Wales. However, the over-emphasis on SEN gradually led to a broader interpretation of inclusion, so that an inclusive school is seen to be one which has both a structure and an ethos within which SEN, gifted and talented, those with English as a second language, males, females, etc. have the opportunity to achieve their potential. For schools, this also means that no learner should be penalized by an inappropriate curriculum provision, and therefore the need for a range of appropriate learning and teaching styles is inevitable.

Personalized learning

This is perhaps the key element, in the UK in particular, in the change in the educational world from expecting learners to fit into the structures and systems as best they can to a provision which meets the individual's personal and specific needs. West-Burnham (2005, p. 23) emphasizes that the personalization of learning is underpinned by 'a deep respect for learners, based on trust and recognition of their value as unique human beings'.

He proposes some core principles, including:

- services designed in response to the defined needs of clients
- clients as partners in the design and development of future provision
- the primary accountability of providers to clients
- clients' ability to make valid, self-directed choices. (2005, p. 16)

Substitute the word 'learners' for 'clients' and these principles illustrate the challenge personalized learning presents to systems which depend on centralized curricula and/or progress according to age. However, the much greater use of individualized data and innovative uses of Information Technology have meant that forward-looking schools have been able to make considerable progress in personalizing learning, even within the above structures. A particular emphasis on learning to learn has liberated many students to be able to determine their own progression routes, supported by trained mentors or coaches. We should also note that for many learners, collaboration will be vital in achieving that (Leadbeater, 2005), because of the need to share resources, human and otherwise.

Workforce reform

This issue is a very specific one to education in England and Wales. The considerable growth of support staff employed in schools in the 1990s, linked closely with the need for teachers to focus on their specialist roles and concern with a general societal anxiety about work–life balance, led ultimately to the strategy (DfES, 2002) enabling schools to reform and restructure the workforce. The implementation of this strategy has enabled schools to examine and develop more creative staffing structures and a report (Ofsted, 2003) found that these included the development of services involving provision before and after the traditional school day. Middlewood et al. (2005, pp. 54–60), in writing about the Learning School, give various examples of these new structures, all based on new approaches to contract design and flexible use of the individual's skills, regardless of official status. Chapter 4 of this book expands on this.

Similarly, in Children's Services, ECM proposed that everyone working with children, young people and families should have a common set of professional skills and knowledge. The common areas of expertise were:

- effective communication and engagement
- the development of children and young people
- the safeguarding and promoting of children's welfare
- the supporting of transitions
- multi-agency working
- the sharing of information
  (DfES, 2005b)

and these would be assessed via a Common Assessment Framework (CAF) (DfES, 2006a).

Partnerships and networking

Since the 1980s, various developments have placed requirements on schools to ensure that they entered into new relationships with stakeholders, so that these became part of the process itself. This opened up ways for new relationships to emerge.

In England and Wales, the Five Year Strategy for Children and Learners (DfES, 2004) underlined the importance of partnerships between schools, communities and parents. In fact, since the early days of the marketization of education and the intense individual competition between schools that followed, collaboration had been endorsed by various initiatives. These included Leading Edge (where a 'successful' school could be linked with ones that needed support) and federations of schools to offer combined services. NCSL's initiatives such as Networked Learning Communities likewise encouraged joint ventures to develop collaborative learning projects at a local level. All these gave official endorsement to what many see as natural to educationalists in the public sector, collaborating for the benefit of the child. In a world of increasing mobility for families, such a notion of collaboration is an important shared value for all concerned.

All the above developments were in place and proceeding at the time when the first proposals for extended schools appeared. We shall see that they are all important elements for any school which is offering effective extended or full-service provision or is aspiring to do so. Along with issues such as environmental sensitivity, sustainability, student/pupil voice and many others which effective schools are already addressing, they form the basis of trying to build integrated relationships with partners and communities which reflect many of these same issues. Without this need to share being acknowledged, any school will always be seen as trying to impose its own values upon communities and partners which may, in a few cases, be directly opposed to them. As our chapter on leadership examines, this is what can make leadership of these schools so risky, even dangerous, and why a new kind of leadership is therefore essential.

The UK proposals and implementation progress

The proposal for extended schools was part of the 2006 paper setting out a ten-year strategy for Sure Start Children's Centres and childcare, as well as for extended schools. This Sure Start initiative closely mirrored the US one – Head Start – as in the USA, it had been clearly acknowledged also that if there were to be 'No child left behind' for future generations, then babyhood, infancy and early childhood were at the heart of effective reform. Family satisfaction, with a particular stress on early intervention, is becoming a measure of effectiveness, with family satisfaction surveys being practised in Belgium (Lanners and Mombaerts, 2000) and piloted in Greece (Kaderoglou and Drossinou, 2005). By 2010, a Sure Start Children's Centre is intended to be in every community in England and Wales, with every school open from 8.00 a.m. to 6.00 p.m. and offering easy access to childcare activities for children, young people and the community, and quick referral to specialist health and social care services.

Additionally, all local early years childminders are to be part of a network linked to a school or Sure Start centre. According to Carpenter (2005), such universal childcare programmes helped the Nordic nations to abolish child poverty by catching potential problems early.

Some of the early reactions to the requirement for schools to be open until 6.00 p.m. were predictable:

'Our members remain committed to the ECM agenda but what we have not signed up to is a national babysitting programme.' (NAHT, April 2006)

'What we can't have is a situation where schools are providing breakfast clubs and after-school clubs on the cheap.' (NUT, April 2006)

Views on progress range, depending upon the 'half-full or half-empty glass' perspective of the person concerned. A survey of headteachers found in April 2006 (*Headspace*, April (47): 2) that 'only 26% were running or planning to run by 2007 a service till 6.00 p.m.; 37% had no plans in place at all; 35% had plans for an unspecified future time'. The Chief Executive of the National Children's Bureau described the progress in England and Wales by 2006, in the context of a ten-year programme, as remarkable and the Chief Executive of 4Children said that with 4000 schools 'signed up', 5000 by 2007, and a further 5000 in hand, the 'critical mass of forty–fifty per cent was near' and there 'will always be thirty per cent who are slow or reluctant but that's only to be expected'.

By 2007, a survey found that 72 per cent of all schools were offering some form of extended schooling – this is evidence of continuing progress towards the target.

What is undeniable therefore is that there already exists a large number of schools in England and Wales offering extended or full-service provision, and an equally large number keen to begin or develop the small starts they have made into better provision. Examples are given throughout the chapters of this book, as well as practical advice drawn from their experience on how to develop further. Drawing on the many excellent examples, from the UK and several other countries, it is possible to highlight some common factors in their effectiveness.

Clear understanding and commitment to purpose

Those committed to providing true extending schooling need to be absolutely clear about its ultimate purpose. We earlier described this as 'transforming communities' and each community served by a particular extended school will be unique. However, all communities are part of wider society and extended schooling should be seen as part of a 'strategy for working towards equity and social justice' (West-Burnham, 2006, p. 102). Grandiose as this may sound, it needs to be embodied in the values and vision established by every individual extended school, because, without an awareness of the ultimate aim of the school, there is a definite risk that some schools will simply have 'extended practice'. This means that they will be open from 8.00 a.m. until 6.00 p.m., and will offer facilities and activities in the extra time. This may be worthwhile in itself and for some schools, it will be a development of current provision but it will remain no more than a school with an 'add-on', unless the values which underpin the additional provision are ones which reach out to the community and engage with its members in that provision.

Whatever new emphasis is given to community engagement, the extended school never loses sight of the fact that its first focus and its daily 'bread and butter' concern remains the child and the child's learning and achievement.

This understanding needs to permeate the school's ethos. This permeation, of course, takes time but, for example, all those appointed to the staff of the school, in whatever role, need to be able to understand and accept the guiding principles of school and community being wholly integrated. Mitchell (2005, p. 6) suggests one of the descriptors of a quality extended service school: 'a situation where involvement by school and community are virtually indistinguishable'. The elements in the evolution of such an ethos will be determined by the needs of the pupils/students, staff, and the community (i.e. all learners). Those teachers appointed to the school staff in specialist roles will have the opportunity to continue to develop their expertise to the greatest degree possible, but they will also recognize that:

- other people contribute to each person's learning, including families
- equal but different expertise exists in those working in other fields, which impacts significantly on the individual's development
- only in partnership with these other contributors can progress in effective learning occur.

A willingness to devolve and share responsibility

Within the school, this will be reflected in a commitment to

- distributed leadership (this and other leadership aspects are dealt with in Chapter 3)
- pupil/student voice.

This is because the school itself is a community for its learners, and as such is an important agent of socialization. The messages received within this community about shared values, social behaviour, norms and attitudes, rights and responsibilities are ones which are carried from school and form part of the crucial interaction between school and community. Learners' rights and responsibilities as useful citizens are an integral part of the ECM agenda, and children and young people need to be much more involved – and see and feel that they are involved – in how their daily lives and learning are managed. While it is true that older students are a more obvious group to participate in school decision-making, our research – and that of others – shows clearly that even very young children are willing to accept and capable of much greater ownership of their learning at school. As far as young people are concerned, the UK paper *Youth Matters – What Next?* (2005) produced a huge response in its consultation, showing that young people were interested and furthermore had a host of good ideas for the provision offered to them.

Community empowerment

Reaching out and listening to the community are essential and later chapters deal with this in more detail. We should note that it is very tempting for schools to impose their views as to what is needed upon the local communities, but it needs to be resisted as firmly as the school resisting every single thing the community says it wants it to do! Using community liaison officers, community development workers, focus groups, surveys and community conferences are all ways in which community needs can be more realistically identified. The notion of 'learning champions' has been effective in several areas of England, to the extent that any centralized adult learning team in some areas has been dispensed with and only those services or programmes which the community learning champions have identified as being needed or requested 'out there' in the community are provided.

A relentless flexibility

Because of the constant changes in education and society as a whole, extended schools need to be prepared all the time to adapt current practice to new needs and priorities and, where necessary, to make some wholesale changes. These adaptations or wholesale changes can include:

- flexibility in people's roles
- flexibility in structuring school days and terms
- flexibility in the organization of learning groups
- flexibility in curriculum provision
- flexibility in the use of technology.

Flexibility in people's roles

With a focus on personalized learning firmly at the centre, the principle for everyone employed in developing pupil/student learning is that everyone is working *with* each other, not *for* each other. The recognition of individual employees comes via a respect for the specialist skills and knowledge they possess. The starting point, as Middlewood and Parker have suggested (2001, p. 202) is '... not "How can I make the teaching more effective here?" ... but rather "How can learning be most effective here?"'. Individual specific roles develop from the answer to that question.

Similarly, in terms of pupil or student personal welfare, a truly inclusive extended school tries to see every situation as a learning situation and staff's life experiences, e.g. as family members, can be used – with training – to give support to a learner, whether their designated role is that of teacher, technician or receptionist. The notion that only subject teachers are able to act as personal tutors to students has already been rejected in many secondary schools in the UK. Specialist support services need to be available and easily and quickly accessible but for the majority of learners, the flexible roles of staff enable everyday needs to be met.

Flexibility in structuring school days and terms

The 'factory model' of start school, lessons, break, lessons, lunch, lessons, etc. is widely seen as completely hostile to the needs of pupils and students in schools committed to personalizing learning. Even within the conventional school day (say 8.30 a.m. to 4.00 p.m.), a number of schools operate a continuous learning day. Simply by staggering break times, not only is learning occurring during formal settings through the day, but the pressure on spaces, on the need for regimented behaviour, for 'crowd control', and on staff placed with the out-of-class learners are all reduced significantly. Equally, the learning of the need to develop a calmer ethos outside the class out of respect for those still learning is a clear example of learning with others, as those outside will be inside at some point and need the same respect!

Likewise, the structure of the school year is increasingly being determined by what are relevant and appropriate 'blocks of effective learning time' rather than by historical precedents, dating back to the nineteenth century in some parts of the UK.

Flexibility in the organization of learning groups

Many educationalists – and increasingly politicians also – are suggesting that certainly in the UK, we shall at some point this century look back with bewilderment at times when our schools were organized around the chronological age of the children, with all those of a certain age moving together from year to year! Personalized learning and assessment for learning all promise an escape from the tyranny of examinations at prescribed ages to assessment at a time when the individual is ready. Thus, groupings will be endlessly flexible; sometimes single gender, sometimes mixed gender, sometimes large numbers, sometimes small numbers, sometimes common interest, sometimes mixed adult/children and sometimes solitary. The extended school offers increased opportunities for some of these possibilities because of the exciting mix of its clients and its recognition of their priorities.

Flexibility in curriculum provision

In personalized learning in inclusive extended schools, the goal is to motivate all learners 'to become active investors in their own learning' (Leadbeater, 2005, p. 9). The key includes improving skills as a learner, and gaining the qualities of responsibility, resilience, resourcefulness and reflection. To this end, the organization of groupings and periods of time spent on a learning activity (above) need to be flexible so that *how* the learning is occurring becomes more central than *what* is being learned.

Flexibility in the use of technology

The 'ownership' principle in extended schools referred to earlier is particularly relevant here, as learners in this century take responsibility for the tools when they regard them as their own. Information technology 'creates a shared platform for learning, linking school, home and community' (Leadbeater, 2005, p. 14), encouraging both personalized and collaborative learning. Technology puts the tools in the learners' hands and so makes them more able to participate. The huge success of the provision of computer classes for senior citizens throughout the developed world is a notable illustration of this.

These factors, along with clear policies and strategies, a realistic timetable for achieving them, and the ability to forge strong effective partnerships with external agencies of all kinds, give a flavour of what an effective extended school is. One final and crucial point must be made in this chapter, however. It is the need to remember that there is no one single model for an extended school – they come in all shapes and sizes! These may include:

- clusters of schools
- a school or schools with agencies and other services close at hand
- the full-service extended school – a 'one-stop' supermarket of services where everybody will find something to suit their needs.

The actual model will depend on many factors, including capacity, location, local community composition and, perhaps above all for leaders and managers, where the school is *now*, so that development can build from that point.

Further reading

Dryfoos, J., Quinn, J. and Birkin, C. (2005) *Community Schools in Action*. Oxford: Oxford University Press.
Piper, J. (2006) *Schools Plus to Extended Schools*. Coventry: ContinYou.

Points to consider

- How confident are you of the degree to which there would be/is support for extended schooling in your organization?
- How well do you really know your local community, its needs, and its potential contribution?
- Using the list given in this chapter, is it possible to do an analysis of where the school is currently in each of the areas dealt with in this chapter?
- Could there be a value in nominating 'learning champions' in the school and/or the community? That actual title does not have to be used. They will need a clear brief but also a free hand to spot opportunities wherever they are for the school or network to contribute to some form of learning.

2

The implications for current schooling

This chapter considers the following questions:

- What kinds of curriculum approaches are needed?
- What changes in management and organization are needed?
- How can links with communities be enhanced?
- What kind of ethos needs to be developed?
- What policies and strategies need to be considered?

For the process and outcomes described in Chapter 1 to be realized, there will need to be significant changes in many aspects of conventional schooling as we have known it. Fortunately, many forward-looking schools in the UK, the United States, Australia, Canada, New Zealand, Holland, Sweden, Norway and Denmark, among others, are already well down this road. We consider some of the areas for change here.

Learning and teaching and the curriculum

In several countries which have highly centralized education systems – for example, China and Greece (see Foskett and Lumby, 2003) – the scope for individual schools or groups of schools to develop their own initiatives is extremely limited. Even in some other countries where delegated or school-based management (SBM) exists, a nationally prescribed curriculum 'can become a serious obstacle rather than a learning opportunity' (MacBeath et al., 2007, p. 17), and, as outlined in Chapter 1, only personalized learning, self-knowledge as a learner and a learning which enthuses the person for life can develop 'a culture in which learning is safe, adventurous and significant to the learner' (p. 19).

Fortunately, despite restrictions and an obsession with inappropriate age-related standardized tests, 'measures and subject straitjackets' (Cousins, 2005, p. 165), there are large numbers of schools encouraging and developing:

- personalized learning
- a spirit of enquiry, reflection and risk-taking
- assessment for learning
- learning to learn.

For these to be fully developed, new models of curriculum are needed where the emphasis is more on process than on content. For examples, see Middlewood et al., 2005, pp. 107–22 and West-Burnham, 2005, pp. 48–58. Such a curriculum must be an inclusive one, defined by Clough and Corbett (2000, p. 164) as a 'workable structure … operating in a dynamic, unpredictable, interactive process'. The use of words such as 'unpredictable' and 'adventurous' give a flavour of the element of risk-taking for school leaders and, undoubtedly, on the journey of development there are times when a straitjacket seems easier! But, there are specific areas of a curriculum where a beginning can be made, for example, ensuring an emphasis in Personal and Social Education on helping and supporting each other. For much of the above to develop, so that an appropriate ethos is fostered, some structures have to be loosened at the very least.

Changes in management and organization

There is divided opinion as to whether the more effective way to bring about organizational change is to begin with structures or with culture. Hargreaves (1997) summarizes the two opposing views:

1 Structures should be changed first so that people's attitudes can be changed as they recognize that they are not contained by those structures but can enact their true values.
2 The culture values should be encouraged to develop first so that people see for themselves that the structures are inhibiting these and need to be changed.

Hargreaves suggests that ultimately something of both is needed, but for the changes we are discussing here, everything depends for leaders and managers on where they are now. If a school is already well advanced in personalizing learning, an inclusive curriculum and seeing learning as more of a journey and less of a destination, the need to get rid of restraining structures will be obvious, despite the fact that they have been there for a long time!

The most obvious change needed is the reorganization of the traditional school day already referred to briefly in Chapter 1. There is nothing more alien to personalizing learning than a prescriptive structure which specifies precise blocks of learning time – punctuated by bells!

Abandoning the bells for some schools has often been a significant step towards signalling to pupils/students and staff that learning goes on all the time and that artificial limits are very unhelpful. Of 16 schools in England (primary and secondary) that we contacted which have given up using bells, every single one was enthusiastic about this and not one was considering reintroducing them. Even one split-site secondary which had had many reservations, for obvious reasons, had found that, after initial problems, the effects were positive. The benefits given were that:

- pupils appreciated the greater trust given them
- staff likewise appreciated the greater trust given them, for themselves and the pupils
- staff in some schools entered into 'trading time' between subjects so that no one lost out
- a less institutionalized ethos was found to develop
- punctuality at classes either improved or stayed the same
- a small environmental benefit was noted (i.e. less noise)
- fire bells were responded to immediately and treated seriously!

The significance of even this change for extended schooling is clear, since the ultimate aim is blurring the distinction between formal statutory time and extended time.

The actual reorganization of the traditional school day has had significant changes flowing from it for several schools. Crossley (2002, p. 3) describes how Kings College, Guildford, decided to operate a continuous school day. Every student has two breaks in the day, one for brunch, one for lunch. In the Cyber Restaurant, there is a seat for everyone who goes at a particular time. Breaks are organized by class with no more than 180 students going at any one time, and … 'breaks often take place *within* lessons and students leave their work on their desks and return after the break. Its significance is dramatic and all-pervading.

- It is a fundamental element of our ethos of trust and culture of achievement.
- Its impact extends well beyond the basics of breaks and catering organization.
- It enables almost unobtrusive adult supervision'.

Crossley also describes how other benefits accrue:

- Consideration for others becomes the by-word.
- Food quality is enhanced, because of catering for smaller numbers at any one time.

- Visitors of all kinds are comfortable and welcome in the restaurant.
- Staff mix with a wider variety of colleagues.

Significantly, he argued that the move to provide additional activities at the end of the conventional school day, rather than in break times, occurred 'in a more natural way'.

It was also found (Crossley, 2003, p. 4), that new ways of organizing learning and teaching inevitably followed and, with technology 'as the servant', the school moved 'to create a situation where the timetabled lesson is simply one of a number of ways where a particular course can be completed … small group tutorials, distance/online learning, video conference or email links to teacher and other guides'.

At another age level altogether, a nursery and infant school in Rushden, Northamptonshire in England found that simply by staggering the times of breaks so that learning was continuous, the youngest and older children gained in:

- more contented and satisfying break times
- fewer 'behavioural incidents' for staff to deal with
- a quieter ethos with more consideration for others
- more effective learning overall.

Another structural change which is essential for effective extended schooling is the breaking down of hierarchies. The traditional model of headteacher → deputies → middle leaders/managers → staff is rendered meaningless by the need for employees *at all levels* to have the facility to take action with a wide range of colleagues and clients inside and outside the boundaries. Although accountability needs to be clear (see Chapter 5), any structure which restricts employees from, for example, developing new community group links by having to check back with a line manager at every stage, will inhibit progress considerably and undermine the community's trust in the school's ability to deliver. Any new structure can only be represented concentrically. It should be stressed that this is only a crude representation.

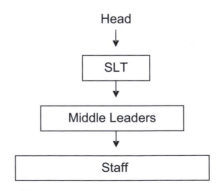

Figure 2.1 Linear structure model

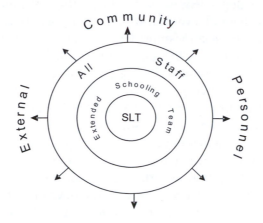

Figure 2.2 Concentric structure model

Far more important than the actual structure are the roles and responsibilities that each employee has in terms of flexibility and autonomy. New ways of organizing staff are needed, as discussed in Chapter 4. One other important reason for becoming much less hierarchical in the actual school is the signal this sends to outsiders, i.e. that you believe in empowerment and autonomy, an essential element in effective integrated community services.

What kind of ethos needs to be developed?

The ethos of an extended or full-service provision school is very different from that of a conventional teaching and learning school. As anyone entering and walking around a school, or indeed any organization, knows, ethos is 'what you see, what you hear, what you feel'. To complete this, we may say on leaving and having experienced that ethos that you 'understand' what the school does, what it stands for, what it believes in, what it is trying to achieve. As more than one school leader told us, the attitude, outlook and behaviour of young people is automatically affected by the new mix of people who are to be encountered on school premises. As one secondary extended school principal memorably expressed it, 'they discover they could easily bump into their neighbour, uncle, auntie, baby nephew or grandma!'.

We have mentioned that it is important to trust and respect partners: trust must be central to the ethos of an extended school, for trust makes sharing, welcoming and accessibility possible.

The move away from hierarchy to a more interdependent structure, recommended earlier, brings with it the need for people to trust each other more, simply because they are more dependent on each other, rather than merely those immediately above or below them in a vertical structure. Any school is a complex network of social interactions and relationships; an extended school is infinitely more so with its web of people operating in a range of specialist, voluntary and other roles. Instead of fixed roles, the 'non-threatening role ambiguity' (Woods, 2005, p. 132) helps to blur divisions between people who find they do not need to hide behind their status as much and can work at whatever level is required. Woods calls this ability to shed status or take it on as appropriate 'status adaptability', and it is acknowledged as one of the joys of people leadership when someone is seen to 'rise to the occasion', i.e. take on the status required for that particular situation.

West-Burnham (2005, p. 104) uses the analogy of the parent/child relationship to illustrate the crucial importance of trust in the development of relationships.

As the trust that parents have in their children grows with age, maturity and confidence, so the transactional nature of their relationship changes, for example:

- there is less permission seeking and giving
- decisions are increasingly delegated
- the demand for detailed accountability diminishes
- the amount of negotiation increases.

In essence, the relationship changes from immature control to mature trust.

The analogy of parent and child is particularly apt because it reminds us that the path to mature trust is not easy and may be fraught at times!

An ethos rooted in the trust people have for each other also has the powerful impulse for social justice, since in the respect for others emerges the recognition of potential or real injustices, for example in the unequal distribution of resources or inequitable treatment of groups or individuals based on prejudice. Trust therefore encourages *sharing*, and Woods (2005) suggests three kinds:

- sharing of authority
- sharing of aspiration and expectation
- sharing of the benefits of actions.

If this seems too idealistic, we need to remind ourselves of the commitment to the ultimate purpose of extended schooling, without which we shall have 'schools with extras' but not transformed communities. We are encouraged by the passion and integrity of those we met during the research for this book which convinces us that such transformation *is* possible.

How can such an ethos be developed? Many reading this book will recognize the ethos described above as already present in their schools and others may wish to take stock of where they are now. Smith (2006, p. 9) suggests five 'quick fixes' that help schools to know if they are ready to begin ECM or develop what they already have further. These are:

- 'identifying a key person within school who will talk to outside agencies
- finding out as much as possible about the external agencies and what they can do to help and support the school
- being open to external agencies visiting schools and encouraging them all to talk to staff and to children
- trying to expand or make changes to personal, social and health education and citizenship so that "helping and supporting each other" becomes part of the school's ethos
- making the importance of all aspects of Every Child Matters obvious by using staff training positively. Invite in police officers, social workers and health professionals to tell everyone what they do and how they can be both helpful and useful.'

Two heads of extended schools, one primary and one secondary, advocated having periods in a school where role reversal was practised. 'Putting yourself in someone else's shoes is a wonderful way of testing out the reality of what is really going on,' said one.

These sessions included:

- the headteacher acting as receptionist for a couple of hours
- teachers being cleaners after school for a day
- pupils planning the visit of a VIP
- using associate staff as classroom teachers, capitalizing on the individual expertise they bring for the learners and many others!

Shadowing individuals or groups of pupils is a well-established method of ascertaining curriculum provision (though not widely practised), but it also offers powerful insights into ethos. One of us will never forget waiting in the rain outside a mobile classroom for a late teacher while shadowing a group. Never have I felt so disruptive! NCSL in England encourages headteachers, teachers and then pupils in a 'Learning Walk' where people from paired schools (and these have included parents and governors) visit each other's places and absorb the atmosphere as a learning experience, seeing and feeling the familiar place through a new pair of eyes. Usually, any changes that result are the simplest kind, arising from straightforward questions:

- 'Why do the staff say *that?*'
- 'Why do the students not go there?'
- 'Why does the head ...?'

Finally, there is the development of pupil or student voice. The extent to which the statutory learners in the school are increasingly involved in the development and ownership of their own learning is fundamental to an ethos which will encourage learners of all ages and all kinds in extended schooling. Whether through school councils, student research, involvement in recruitment and selection, the engaging in assessment of their own learning and indeed the teaching they receive, experience is showing that such developments – for all ages of children – bring confidence to all those involved, raise personal esteem and, crucially for extended schooling, demonstrate how learners can be trusted to take control of their own learning.

Recently, at a full-service extended school in Leicester, students were given the responsibility of the whole process of selecting the person to be the new student manager. They carried out all the interviews, and made their recommendation to the principal and governors, which was accepted without question. The school's argument was that this was a post which the students would be most affected by and they had complete trust in the students' ability to appoint someone appropriate. Of course, this situation is not arrived at quickly but it gives an idea of the potential that lies in enabling student voice to be a more proactive and integral feature of school life.

How can schools' links with communities be enhanced?

In the new context for schools outlined in Chapter 1, the notions of collaboration and partnerships as being a crucial element of the schools' response to this context was made clear. If schools are to develop into areas with integrated services for and with their communities, we suggest there may be five steps to consider in this development:

  (i) know and understand the communities
 (ii) draw the communities into working in partnership with the school
(iii) work with the communities to help identify their needs
(iv) ensure the schools are welcoming and accessible
 (v) trust and respect the communities.

(i) Know and understand the communities

Knowing what kind of community the school serves, at a superficial level, is quite straightforward. In location, it may be anywhere from inner city to suburban to small town to semi-rural to relatively isolated. In material terms, it will be somewhere perhaps on a continuum from extremely deprived to very prosperous, with many categories somewhere between these extremes. School leaders already know this and recognize the issues related to the individual situation, such as transport difficulties in many rural communities, or admissions from outside the zone or catchment area.

However, understanding the communities goes deeper than this kind of awareness, with its assumption of a community as relatively homogenous. Using Strike's (2000) categorization of four types of communities (as tribes, as congregations, as orchestras and as families), Bottery (2004, pp. 173–4) suggests that community schools (and extended schools, therefore) need to be somewhere between the two ends of a continuum of Strike's types, 'having different weaknesses, different strengths, depending upon where on this continuum they were situated'. Naive plans about empowering, enabling or democratizing local communities can be made if there are assumptions about them having completely shared values or beliefs. Many if not most communities, for example, will have the potential for inequality in the groups in them:

- inequalities *within* each stakeholder group
- inequalities *between* each stakeholder group.

And, as Wood points out, while there is power which is visible and which may be negotiated or aligned with, there is also '*invisible* power which threads itself through relationships, cultural symbols and everyday patterns of social living' (Woods, 2005). Thus, leaders need to strenuously avoid generalized assumptions about the communities that their schools serve and the groups and individuals that comprise them. They need to remind themselves that not everyone actually wants to be there in the first place! In a series of interviews with local residents carried out by Kerry, a social worker in Nottingham, the answers to the question 'How did you come to be living here?' included:

- 'I was born and bred here, and my parents before me.'
- 'I came here for work thirty years ago, stayed and will die here.'
- 'We moved here as a young couple but hate it now, but can't escape.'
- 'What makes you think we *chose* to come here? We were put here.'
- 'I don't know. Who would choose to live in a dump like this?'

All these people (from nonagenarians to teenagers), as Kerry pointed out to us, were part of the same community, served by one secondary and four primary schools!

A further understanding may be a recognition of the current trend of the community – is it on a downward spiral, decaying? Is it resurgent after a period of neglect? Is it complacent? This judgement needs a knowledge of local history and exploring this in itself, such as through senior citizens, can be both rewarding and give helpful insight to aid one's analysis.

Remember also that communities are always evolving and are doing so as the extended school develops. Long-serving staff at the school can be an invaluable asset in recognizing local issues, sometimes even recognizing the actual families!

(ii) Draw the communities into working in partnership with the school

Each of the agencies, groups or individuals in the communities will eventually need to see themselves as working in partnership with the school(s), so it is worthwhile clarifying one's understanding of this. Pugh's (1989, p. 80) definition is a useful starting point. The parties operate:

> in a working relationship that is characterised by a shared sense of purpose, mutual respect and the willingness to negotiate. This implies a sharing of information, responsibility, skills, decision making and accountability.

People can be justifiably suspicious of being encouraged to enter into partnerships unless they are clear about their own roles and relative positions regarding negotiations, compromise, authority and resources, and of course possible hidden agendas. Knowing that a school will receive government funding if it enters into particular partnerships may make some potential partners either sceptical of true motives or relish the strength of their own position.

Rudd et al. (2003) found in their research into partnerships that these could be 'horizontal' (where members are on an equal footing) or 'vertical' (where one partner shares expertise with another who lacks that expertise). Some factors in partnership effectiveness included:

- clear and realistic aims and objectives
- trust, honesty and openness between partners, with realism about one's own strengths and weaknesses
- a 'bottom-up' approach, taking account of everyone's views
- a sense of ownership by those involved.

The issues faced by schools in partnerships included:

- a fear of the unknown
- a perceived scrutiny by outsiders
- the need to be flexible and willing to compromise.

With an awareness of what different partnerships may involve, the identification of potential partners becomes possible. As will be seen from community and extended schools' experience, described in detail in Chapters 7 and 8, the possibilities are limitless. Simply listing some formal groupings gives some indication:

- business and commercial (local banks, local supermarkets, retailers, manufacturers)
- public service agencies (notably health, police, social care)
- established groups (youth clubs, adult education, sports clubs, Scouts/Guides, etc.)
- local groups (residents, faith groups, ethnic minority groups, etc.)
- other much more loosely formed, even unofficial groups.

Such a list only hints at possibilities and does not take into account all the informal networks that already exist in any community.

In the UK, the existence of the Specialist Schools and Academies Trust, to which the majority of secondary schools belong (and primary schools are also being piloted) actually enhances schools' opportunities in this field, as it is a basic feature of specialist schools' status that they should be involved in community partnerships. Maynard (2007, p. 18) claims that 'specialist schools have been shadowing the emergence of the extended schools' agenda since the late 1990s' and 'a commitment to the principles of inclusion, equal opportunity and cross-cultural provision is inherent' (ibid.). Whatever the merits of school specialism, it is a fact that allocated funding exists for a 'community element' and, using the particular specialism, a start has been made in that area, whether it be in languages, engineering, science, arts, business and enterprise, etc.

So what may draw potential partners into considering working with the school(s)? It would be foolish to ignore the 'what's in it for me?' factor that exists in every partnership – after all, schools have it too! Schools have the advantage of already being local family hubs because children go there every day. In general, they are seen as reliable, trustworthy places and, certainly at primary level, conveniently situated for many families. They are also seen as having a range of spaces and facilities which are known about, even if only through children bringing accounts of them home. So, identifying the needs of potential partners is crucial. Chapters 7 and 8 deal fully with the issue of creating and sustaining such partnerships.

(iii) Work with the communities to help identify their needs

It is essential to remember that the ECM agenda is not about extended schools *competing* with the existing provision but *complementing* services in the community. For example, in childcare, where local services may be offered by the private and the voluntary sectors, for the school to offer childcare at below-market rate would be counterproductive by skewing the market. If other providers go out of business, the net result is a decrease in provision and less choice for parents – let alone the huge damage done to the school's reputation through the resentment of local providers with whom schools may wish to work in other areas. The school leaders who see a provision somewhere in the local community as sketchy and realize it could be done better and more efficiently at the school would be well advised to count to ten before immediately setting up a 'superior' service at the school! The messages provided by the quick, unthinking, if well-meaning, response are:

- 'we are the experts; you are not'
- 'we are superior'
- 'we know what you need'
- 'you will fit in with our ways.'

The following two examples show more effective ways.

Case Example 2.1

Jamie, a youth worker in Derby, tells the story of the school that discovered a group of about a dozen 14–16-year-old boys playing improvised football on a piece of industrial waste ground. It offered the boys the opportunity to come to the school and use the all-weather surface once a week for an hour with a trained coach – free of charge. At first, all attended but numbers quickly fell away and, despite warnings that a minimum number was essential, the initiative collapsed. When asked by Jamie why they had not attended, the reply was, 'We don't want to play when *you* want us to!' Here the listening failed to come before the action. It is possible that the school could not have given the boys what they wanted of course, but at least the image of the superior provider would not have been implanted in their minds.

Case Example 2.2

A good example of complementary provision is in Birmingham where Carl, unemployed in his early twenties, joined a training scheme at a local community school for youth link workers. When qualified, on his own initiative he set up a support group for teenagers in a former estate unit, helping youngsters off the street. He has full autonomy but support when he needs it.

Far from seeing the school as a competitive site, extending schooling is about ensuring integrated services exist in a whole range of appropriate locations. This appropriateness may relate to geographical convenience and transport issues, but also to wariness about meeting certain others. For example, on-site support for pupils or parents with drug problems could deter some through embarrassment of meeting others. Often, as suggested earlier, community link workers may be best placed to help community members identify their needs.

Many leaders we met had found this wariness of actual school sites a deterrent in early days and that going out to reach the client on their own or neutral territory was essential. Nazia, a project manager for the Keighley extended schools cluster in Bradford, chose to 'develop a programme of outreach provision for summer holiday activities, in places where children chose to congregate out of school hours – places that were convenient to them, in public spaces such as parks and other open settings'. Key partners were involved including a community centre, recreation centre, childcare services and parks and landscapes staff. (Hussein, 2008, p. 7). The simplicity of this early initiative with the feedback on the enjoyment the families – and providers – received from it paved the way for significant developments in other projects that the cluster has since developed.

Communities clearly are not static and, as they change, so do their needs. One issue identified by some coordinators was that, occasionally, by the time a consultation (required for funding) had been done, the original group which identified the needs had 'moved on' and the needs were now different.

(iv) Ensure the schools are welcoming and accessible

Schools have become much more welcoming institutions in the last twenty years, despite the inevitable extra security measures which have to be taken for the safety of those within. Welcome boards, often personalized, videos, plasma screens in reception showing pupils in action, information about out of hours activities are now common features of many schools in the UK, the USA, Canada, Australia, New Zealand and some European countries. The skill in accessibility lies in security being seen as of great importance, without being oppressive or hostile. Most public organizations have had to face the same problems without setting up extensive physical barriers. Perhaps the two essentials are:

- information – excellent signposting is still far from universal!
- 'customer care' training for all staff who come into contact with visitors. This training needs to be regularly updated and not merely provided as a response when something goes wrong. Get feedback from visitors just as good hotels do. It need only be on a random basis but two or three dissatisfied or lost visitors are too many!

Too many school foyers seem to the visitors to be dominated by 'late' students, miscreant or ill ones, and interchanges which do not show the best side of an organization. Most of the solutions to these are simple, but the impact is considerable, a point expanded on in Chapter 9.

(v) Trust and respect these partners

Sergiovanni (1996, p. 15) said that we needed to acknowledge 'the capacity of parents, teachers, administrators, and students to sacrifice their own needs for causes they believe in'. This is not easy but, as Bottery (2004, pp. 208–9) argues, without the sacrifice of the parochial for the sake of the bigger cause or belief in education, the development of such causes for greater social justice cannot work. He points out that a school and its leaders, committed to social justice, rise above the personal in a search for 'the building of a constituency which builds values and support between people'. Idealistically, the commitment is to a belief that people do grow while 'being served' so that they become capable of becoming servers themselves. In the meantime, trust and respect – with all the risk-taking and acceptance of failure this implies – become the basis for everything in the partnership.

Policies and strategies to be considered

Dyson (2006, p. 99), drawing on evaluation studies of extended schools in the UK, suggests that there may be two different strategies for school leaders, based on their separate starting points:

- a focus on what local people lack or cannot do and trying to change 'these negative or dysfunctional aspects of individuals or families';
- a focus on the disadvantaging conditions and limited opportunities, and trying to change 'these external circumstances rather than the people themselves'.

While, ideally, extended schools should perhaps be addressing both of these, it is understandable and desirable that one or the other may take precedence, according to the pragmatic needs of the local community. Thus, the absence of a facility leading to the provision of that facility may be the most urgent action needed, prior to working with community members in understanding how to make best use of such provision. So although working opportunistically is not only tempting but sometimes essential, Dyson proposes that aims and purposes need to be thought through carefully, as we suggested as the first priority in Chapter 1, so that initiatives become sustainable.

Strategies for what?

One way of deciding which strategies are needed for what and what the priorities are is to identify the *barriers to achievement and social inclusion*, as perceived locally. A brainstorming of delegates at an Extended Schools Workshop in March 2007 quickly identified thirty such barriers across the schools and communities represented, with no one claiming that every single one existed in an individual place. Analysis suggested that, of these thirty, *nine* might be identified as ones which the school(s) could and should take the lead in developing strategies for, in order to overcome these barriers to achievement and social inclusion:

- bullying
- poor attendance
- a low commitment to homework
- staff with low expectations
- poor relationships in school
- poor provision for children with sensory impairment
- poor provision for severely disabled children
- a poor diet
- a lack of community facilities.

There were fifteen other barriers which were seen as requiring joint school–community action:

- low levels of pre-school literacy
- a high percentage of children bused to school
- high levels of adults with no formal qualifications
- anti-social behaviour (including criminal)
- young carers
- English not spoken at home
- bereavement
- a high teenage pregnancy rate
- a culture of substance misuse (by parent/carers as well as children)
- poor parenting
- poor provision for transient children
- poor provision for looked-after children
- debt
- obesity through inactivity
- the isolation of families and/or individuals.

The other six barriers were seen as ones which the community could address in the long term:

- significant unemployment
- a high percentage of low birth weight
- poverty
- high eligibility for free school meals
- poor housing
- children with a medical condition.

This is, of course, simply an example. It is not a question of agreeing with this list (although most can recognize many of these barriers) or with the analysis. Identifying barriers can only ever be a start and, as Clough and Corbett (2000) suggest, other previously unseen barriers have a way of emerging. The biggest obstacles of all may be people's attitudes and their 'underestimation of their abilities' (p. 105). What we are saying is that by identifying the barriers to achievement and social inclusion in communities, the pressure is on leaders and managers to try to develop strategies which will be seen as:

- relevant
- pragmatic
- visibly effective
- sustainable.

Without the sustainability, faith in what extended schools try to achieve can very quickly be lost. The above form of analysis can also be helpful, in that strategies in which the school itself takes a lead demonstrate that the conventional schooling side of the partnership is showing it can deliver, but that the majority of barriers can only be overcome via integrated community services, and perhaps 'out there' is a vision that the long-term barriers can be overcome by the community's transformation – the ultimate purpose of extended schools. (Further discussion of potential barriers to effective partnerships is explored in Chapter 7.)

This example might be used as part of an overall plan for developing extended schooling. It is crucial to have the big picture, based on the ultimate key purpose, as stated in Chapter 1. Table 2.1 shows how it might operate.

Table 2.1 Approaching extended schooling (based on Woodland, 2007)

Action	Purpose
Data collection	To understand the community
Data analysis	To identify needs
Deciding on strategic direction	To assess what services may be needed and the possible role school(s) may play in providing them
Resource analysis	To assess what resources will be needed and what new ways of service delivery may be required
Drawing up partnership list	To identify possible or essential organizations, partners, collaborators needed
Fixing the vision	To identify a realistic end vision, involve architects where necessary and prepare documentation
Prioritizing implementation activities	To structure and prioritize implementation actions and establish outline costs for early projects.

📖 Further reading

Middlewood, D., Parker, R. and Beere, J. (2005) *Creating a Learning School*. London: Paul Chapman Publishing.

Parker-Jenkins, M., Hewitt, D., Brownhill, S. and Sanders, T. (2007) *Aiming High: Raising the Attainment of Pupils from Culturally Diverse Backgrounds*. London: Paul Chapman Publishing.

West-Burnham, J. and Coates, M. (2005) *Personalising Learning*. Stafford: Network Educational Press.

Points to consider

- How do you ensure everyone visiting the school is made to feel welcome? How do you know?
- Could bells be abolished in your school? If not, why not?
- Is it worth considering a 'brainstorming' session in an open forum, identifying the pluses and then the barriers to achievement in the locality? Perhaps do one first within the school, to familiarize staff with the process and also to compare results later.
- Would it be worthwhile attempting a 'putting yourself in someone else's shoes' trial? For example, could one of the leadership team find out what it is like to do a receptionist's job for half a day?

3

What kinds of leadership then?

This chapter considers the following questions:

- Does the extended school require a radically different style of leadership?
- What are the key requirements for extended school leaders?
- Are some leadership styles particularly suited to leading extended schools successfully?
- What are the major implications facing school leaders of extended schools?

A totally different approach?

The DfES/PricewaterhouseCoopers' Report (2007) on school leadership in the UK cited Workforce Remodelling, Every Child Matters and the 14–19 curriculum agenda as having the greatest impact on school leaders' roles. They considered the following factors to be crucial:

- the need for a more strategic approach
- changing the traditional ethos and culture of the school
- embracing a more diverse workforce
- developing new networks with a range of external organizations
- a new focus on negotiating skills
- developing expertise in facilities and contract management
- consulting with the wider community
- simultaneously continuing to focus on the maintenance and improvement of educational outcomes.

These factors closely mirror what will be needed for the leadership of extended schools. School leaders will have far less time to concentrate on operational matters. It will be a prerequisite that they have the time, the support and the professional development necessary to help create and sustain the vision and direction setting, meet and deal effectively with a far greater range of stakeholders, make the appropriate organizational changes and maintain a clear and rigorous emphasis on what makes for effective teaching and learning for *all* learners.

Many of the skills needed to run any organization will be used in running extended schools. So-called conventional transactional leadership models where school leaders have been autocratic and centralist in approach may have worked in part fifty years ago, but as schools have become larger, more multi-functional and increasingly open to public scrutiny, so school leaders have had to look at more open and democratic models for leading their schools. When Davies (2005, p. 2) makes the observation that 'leadership is about direction setting and inspiring others to make the journey to a new and improved state' and that it 'is not the provenance of one individual but of a group of people who provide leadership in the school and, by so doing, provide support and inspiration to others', few would disagree. However, in leading and managing extended schools, where the child is placed at the heart of the service provision, the implications of these observations become much more keenly defined.

The DfES/PricewaterhouseCoopers' Report (2007) also suggested possible changes in the *structure* of leadership of schools, especially where one person leads a number of schools; they go on to comment that this person could be in a chief executive role, and may not necessarily be an educationalist. This could seem particularly relevant to an extended schools network but there is strong evidence from several developed countries that changing structures does *not* bring better outcomes. Our contention therefore is that it is the quality of the leader or leaders that is the most significant factor and since we believe extended schooling is about everyone being a learner, the leaders must be focused on that.

The task facing the leaders of today's schools is to recognize and respond effectively to the fact that the ECM agenda requires a much greater range of services to work together to create and sustain the right context in which all children can develop their potential and become motivated, articulate and socially adept young citizens. The extent to which schools are successful will in large measure be down to the quality of school leadership. School leaders will need to move the focus away from school improvement primarily in terms of educational outcomes to a much broader perspective – one that considers the whole needs of the child. A society that demands constant and rigorous testing of its young people must recognize that *every child measured is not the same as every child matters*!

Essential requirements: different not more!

What is needed therefore from those who are signed up to the philosophical and pedagogical thinking driving the extended schools' initiative is a great deal of courage and an unswerving commitment to the principle. Leaders of extended schools will be passionate about the opportunities for growth and influence these schools will have, and will not be easily persuaded or deterred by the inevitable voices urging them to draw back from an initiative that appears to be putting even more pressures on them and rendering them ever more accountable.

An understandable initial response from those who are yet to be convinced by the arguments put forward for extended schools might well be to ask how on earth it is possible or indeed reasonable to expect headteachers to take on all this additional responsibility and survive – after all, don't they already have too much to do? The figures regularly paraded showing the number of existing headteachers in the UK and in several other countries leaving the profession early, and the reluctance of the vast majority of the workforce to step up and replace them, may well be a clear signal to political leaders and thinkers that enough is enough! This apparent reluctance to become a headteacher/principal is by no means a UK phenomenon. The reaction from the general secretary of the UK's National Association of Head-teachers to a report proposing a legal extension of the school day once a week was significant when he maintained that putting children in a kind of prison once a week would not go down well with his colleagues and highlighted some of the concerns voiced about the thinking behind extended schools.

Kenny Frederick, a London headteacher and leading exponent of FSES, puts forward the counter argument when she says (*TES*, 2006, p. 21):

> The point is that heads and teachers do not have to do it all. They need to allow others to lead, to share responsibility with support staff and other agencies and professionals. We need to work to develop community leadership so that the community can provide its own safety net for vulnerable young people and not be dependent on the professionals.

These views are not advocating an entirely new way of running schools. They are not asking headteachers to take on yet more responsibility themselves without any additional resources or guidance. They are, however, stating very clearly that leaders of extended schools will have to re-examine their current roles and accept the fact that conventional leadership styles on their own will not allow them to run extended schools without running themselves into the ground! In order to help headteachers, their staff and their governing bodies to approach the task of leading an extended school effectively, the following points need to be kept at the centre of any current and future thinking.

- Many successful school leaders already employ a range of strategies when leading and managing their schools which will be equally effective when leading extended schools.

- Leading extended schools does not automatically mean that headteachers will have to take on more responsibility. Instead, they will have to delegate and empower others to lead – or they will inevitably fail to lead anything.
- Headteachers and governing bodies will have to be comfortable with the fact that there will be agencies operating on their site which will have their own leadership and management structures and separate bosses to whom they are accountable.
- The partnerships which will operate at the centre of extended schools will sit at the heart of the school's thinking and practice and affect it in every dimension. In no sense will their contribution be peripheral or bolt on.
- Although individual performances in terms of public examinations, league tables, etc. will remain a focus, the major driving force for extended schools will be promoting personalized learning and nurturing deep-seated citizenship skills (described by some educationalists as social capital).

What are the implications?

Reference has been made earlier to the fundamental change implicit in the UK government's proposals to make all schools extended schools by 2010. In setting this agenda, and by championing the Every Child Matters philosophy as key to the success of their proposals, the UK government has set itself an immensely demanding task, set as it is within an extremely tight deadline. Their proposals highlight three broad areas as being the yardstick by which the success of this initiative will be measured:

- improved outcomes for children and families
- greater benefits for staff and services
- an increased fit between the services offered and those required by young people and families (DfES, 2005a).

The only way this challenge is going to be met successfully is if school leaders are convinced that the changes will be positive and beneficial and will not place further demands on a leadership workforce which has already felt overwhelmed by the pace and variety of change. MacBeath et al. (2007, p. 13) stress the fact that although schools can achieve a lot in terms of personal and academic achievement, they cannot do it alone:

> If *every* child matters, then there has to be more than the temporary relief offered by 15,000 hours spent in the classroom. If every child is to have a genuine opportunity to gain qualifications and meet the five DfES outcomes (staying healthy, enjoying and achieving, keeping safe, contributing to the community and social and economic well-being), there has to be not only a

concerted provision of services to children and families but a more imaginative response to the multiplicity of disadvantages faced by young people and their families.

The degree to which school leaders will feel empowered to take on the leadership of extended schools will depend on three vitally important factors:

1 Proper advice and guidance on how to address the issues and potential difficulties associated with multi-agency working.
2 Targeted training and support, where necessary, on how to manage and feel comfortable with the principles and practice of distributed leadership.
3 Sufficient capital and associated funding to finance the changes necessary to accommodate the demands of making a campus more accessible more often to very many more users.

At the time of writing, the UK government's response to the funding implications created by the extended school agenda (DfES, 2005a) are not especially encouraging. Although they describe the sums quoted as 'considerable', the actual figures – £50 million in 2003–5, £110 million in 2005–6, £194 million in 2006–7 and £238 million in 2007–8 – pale into insignificance when set against the capital funding of £6 billion a year that is supporting the Building Schools for the Future programme.

It is clear that extended schools will require different types of leadership; they will almost certainly need leaders who are quite unlike the conventional models of the past that have been proposed in the past and which may or may not have proved successful in moving schools forward. It is likely that certain leadership styles will be more effective than others in taking on the particular challenges presented by the extended school agenda – styles that we need to explore in a little more detail.

The enthusiast

Obviously, it is vital that any leader of an extended school is wholly committed to the principle. Leaders of such organizations need to see the concept of wraparound (full-service) schooling as widening the perspective of an already clearly established ethos and pedagogical philosophy. For example, we know of a headteacher of a school in South Yorkshire who was determined to establish the extended school ethos at the heart of his school. After only two years, it has become a copy book 'how-to-do-it' guide for extended services, with breakfast clubs and drop-in sessions for parents, children and adolescents. It has trainee social and health workers on site and has just opened its own sports facility. Under the head's leadership, the school has raised funds for its sports complex from sources including the local authority, the Football Foundation and a series of concerts over three years. It now offers adult fitness classes as well as school swimming lessons – even children's parties – and stays open during the holidays. While income from the external facilities cross-subsidize the school, its own funds are safe-guarded. Likewise, the extra staff who are taken on are paid from the income they generate. This gives the head-teacher greater flexibility and a wider pool of expertise.

It is unlikely that safe conventional textbook actions would have achieved all this – the headteacher in this example had to utilize a wide and disparate set of strategies to secure all this in such a short time.

However, we have already noted that the idea of schools extending their roles and responsibilities in this way excites strong views. A report in *The Times* (Frear, 2007) following a piece of research carried out by the University of Oxford and The Institute of Fiscal Studies gave examples of strong reactions from professionals about the rights and wrongs of formal childcare. A spokesman at the 2007 Annual Conference of The Association of Teachers and Lecturers (ATL) said that she was concerned about the pressures on parents to use wraparound childcare and that it is the parents who should be wrapping their children in their arms and not expecting other people to do it for them. This argument, presenting as it does a clear line of thinking that challenges parents to recognize their own responsibilities, is an argument that will need to be met with conviction and vigour by leaders who understand that extended schools will have to operate as organizations that are supporting and enhancing family life, not replacing it.

Becoming a full-service school should empower leaders to share their vision of what makes for the most effective teaching and learning with all relevant stakeholders. Frequently in this book, we make reference to new, more dynamic partnerships being at the heart of the extended school. School leaders will need to make a profound reassessment of a school's role and ask key questions:

- What is a learner?
- What are the school's relationships with its community?
- How will it work with its customers and service providers?
- What is the precise nature of this new relationship and how can potential partners be convinced that operating on a school site is both a natural and sensible business move?
- How do we ensure that these partnerships are equally valid and valuable to those involved?

Even the language is new!

In order to take on these new challenges, school leaders will have to be convinced that the positive effects of extended schooling on the quality of learning operating at the heart of the organization will be transparently powerful. Deciding to embrace this initiative requires a radical re-interpretation of core values – a point made by Bond and Farrar (2005, p. 4):

> Parents and students will move from being consumers of school to co-creators of a learning experience. Schools will no longer be enclosed communities within the community but will be the hubs through which community needs, aspirations and planning are rooted. Schools will no longer be seen solely as guardians of young people at different stages of their development but will take their place as fully fledged, adult shapers of community life.

These observations lie at the very centre of the extended schools philosophy. School leaders, supported by fully supported governing bodies, need to believe the rhetoric in order to establish the practice!

The entrepreneur

Recently, in the vast literature on school leadership, a great deal has been said (e.g. Anderson, 2000) about a relatively new concept: the entrepreneurial head. In some ways, the first case example below illustrates the qualities needed to be an entrepreneur, namely the ability to see a way through a problem, the courage to take risks, the shrewd eye for detail, the business acumen, etc. In another way, it illustrates the difficulty of trying to find a simple definition of what we mean by the entrepreneurial head, because it is highly unlikely that the head in this case example ever had any training to behave in the way he did or would interpret his actions as being those of a man who was determined to do whatever it took to solve the problem – but then perhaps that single-minded bloody-mindedness is part of the skill set as well!

Case Example 3.1

A headteacher of a failing school in Manchester had been unsuccessfully seeking financial support from the local authority to address the state of his school buildings, all of which were in need of being radically refurbished or rebuilt. He was informed by local authority officials that there was limited capital expenditure available and that several schools in the vicinity had prior claim since they were in an even more parlous state. The only factors in his favour were the amount of surplus land the school possessed and the fact that his school was in the middle of a large working-class residential area. This particular head decided to spend the last £8000 of his maintenance budget on an independent health and safety survey which judged the school buildings to be totally unfit for purpose.

continued

continued

The head met with senior officials from the city council and proposed that they either allowed him to sell off part of his surplus land or he would, on health and safety grounds, give his parents notice that he was closing the school. He was immediately granted permission to look for potential buyers. Within two weeks, he had sold the land to a leisure consortium. However, rather than asking for cash, he asked them to build him a new school. They were delighted to accept the terms. The school was built in just eleven months and was open for business by the start of the new academic year. Within two years, the school was judged to be the most rapidly improved school in the county. It became consistently and heavily over-subscribed.

It is easy to see how these skills would be put to good use leading and managing an extended school. To be entrepreneurial, a leader needs to be a good manager, an accomplished organizer, have a keen business sense and, as the case example shows, possess plenty of initiative and courage and be willing to take risks. This inclination to risk-taking is emphasized by Hentschke and Caldwell (2007, p. 150): 'Although it is fashionable to treat tolerance for risk as a generalised leadership virtue, entrepreneurs take this to a level not common to most educators. Entrepreneurs are willing to place their personal as well as professional well-being at risk to achieve their aims. Business success or failure is much more closely associated with personal success or failure.'

Hentschke and Caldwell (2007) also make the point that entrepreneurs more naturally respond to the creation and growth of innovative alternative forms of schooling because these new forms foster the growth of provider options, that is, they reduce the barriers to entry for entrepreneurs who seek to create additional schooling options. Instinctively, therefore, entrepreneurs will view a development like extended schools as a tremendous opportunity, not a threat.

School leaders who are naturally entrepreneurial are not precious or dogmatic about schools and how they operate. They are always looking for new and better, easier ways of doing things and thus instinctively look at the extended schools initiative as presenting many more opportunities than threats. They would also welcome the possibility of working with a much broader client base. When one headteacher noted for his entrepreneurialism talked about the need on occasions to rise above his principles in order to achieve a particular objective, he was not selling out. Rather, he was articulating an increasingly common view that in today's climate, schools being safe, solid and predictable may gain you respect from some quarters. What it will probably not do, however, is open up funding streams, secure new accommodation, create new partnerships, find the right teacher at the right time, or give you the self-belief and the imagination to approach with confidence initiatives as demanding as the extended schools agenda.

The maverick

As with entrepreneurialism, the term 'maverick' has become increasingly familiar in the last few years, although it is nonetheless a similarly difficult concept to define. This leadership style has in some part been the product of the flexibility, autonomy and freedom presented to heads and governing bodies since school-based management or self-governing schools became prevalent in the UK, Canada, the USA, Australia and New Zealand.

Maverick leaders have five defining qualities.

- They are passionate about what they do and demonstrate this passion by a natural, highly developed competitive streak.
- They are intuitively anti-bureaucratic.
- They do not respond well to being given directives from a central authority.
- They enjoy taking risks, albeit calculated ones, and think on their feet.
- They will not tolerate what they perceive to be deliberate under-performance from anyone involved in the organization.

There are real similarities between the maverick and the entrepreneur, not least their natural inclination to think laterally and take risks. However, perhaps there is a little more of the street fighter in the maverick leader. Their natural tendency to confront authority and their innately competitive personalities mean that they will often do whatever it takes (short of being unprofessional) to achieve their aims.

Case Example 3.2

During the teacher recruitment crisis in the UK in the late 1990s, a headteacher working in a deprived school in the West Midlands was facing dire staff shortages a few weeks before the start of the new academic year. Along with fifteen equally desperate heads, he began attending video-conferencing events organized by the local authority where prospective applicants from Australia, New Zealand, the USA and Canada were being interviewed. He was, along with several of his colleagues, eventually extremely impressed with four potential applicants from Canada that they interviewed one Thursday afternoon. He knew that his colleagues would be looking to offer them positions. This particular head worked out that if he stayed up and phoned them at 2.00 a.m. the following morning, they would just be getting ready to go to work. All four readily accepted posts at his school. The other headteachers realized later in the day that on this occasion they had been out-manoeuvred.

At the height of the same teacher recruitment crisis in the UK, one headteacher was finding it almost impossible to find good science teachers. In order to ensure that he did not dilute the quality of his teaching staff, he unilaterally elected to stop teaching the science curriculum statutorily laid down by central government. 'I couldn't find any decent chemistry teachers so we stopped teaching chemistry – better no chemistry at all than chemistry badly delivered' was the sentiment he expressed to the inspectors who visited his school. Although they couldn't officially support his actions, it was clear they applauded his motives. This ability to be governed by guiding principles that are not the slaves of external directives allows leaders to respond to major initiatives like Extended Schools by promoting strategies that make sure the benefits are positively exploited and the pitfalls avoided. And at the heart of the actions taken, there is a real determination to ensure that the quality of service being provided as a result is enhanced.

Leaders of extended schools will frequently have to take decisions on occasions that do not fit into any training manual. The staffing implications alone are huge! Those headteachers who worry overmuch about conventional methods of taking on staff and who may be bound by the current bureaucracy regarding conditions of service, service contracts, etc. may find the need for imagination and flexibility in the way in which staff are deployed difficult to deal with, let alone the complexities of working effectively with other agencies. Nevertheless, it is a fact that numbers of headteachers and principals do achieve all this. (For example, see Middlewood et al. (2005), Chapter 4 on staffing, contracts, etc.)

The politician

As already stated, a major innovation presented by the Extended Schools initiative is building and sustaining positive working relationships with a range of different agencies operating on the same site. If the leadership of the school does not manage this well, then this central objective will not be achieved. A report published by the National College for School Leadership (Coleman, 2006a, p. 44) drew attention to the specific challenges of multi-agency leadership:

> A particular demand within multi-agency leadership centres on the increased political dimension of this activity. Within this context, the notion of politics is concerned with the ways in which decisions are made within groups. Multi-agency working creates a number of particular demands for leaders in relation to the approaches they use to establish and develop relationships with partner agencies. These include developing an effective understanding of different professional cultures and stimulating a collective understanding of the priorities to be addressed.

Leaders of extended schools will need to be politically astute both in the local and wider sense. They will need to be adept at dealing with the multiplicity of issues which inevitably arise when dealing with external agents, including those with a commissioning role and those with a vested interest in becoming dynamic partners in the organization. A key characteristic of political leadership is the ability to keep up to date and speed with local, regional and national initiatives and developments and be equipped to sift the important from the trivial or mundane. Above all, the skill to maintain a strategic distance from the sheer volume of potential admin- istrivia, bureaucracy and detail which inevitably accompanies collaborative partnerships and prioritize accurately what should and should not occupy a leader's time is absolutely essential. As one headteacher observed, 'It can be seductively easy, when dealing with a wide and divergent group of different agencies who have their own agendas and individual needs, to spend far too much time counting the peb- bles and end up missing the beach'.

Paton and Vangen (2004) in their examination of what is meant by political lead- ership introduce the idea of 'collaborative thuggery', which they consider to be an integral part of working effectively with a number of different partnerships. They talk of holding people to account, manipulating agendas and using tough love on occasions to achieve their objectives. They also draw attention to the need for weed- ing as well as nurturing in a garden. What seems to be clear from this analogy is their assertion that leading an extended school does mean that, although there will be many occasions when diplomacy is called for, there will also be times when the gloves have to come off.

Key questions a political leader will ask when addressing the challenges of lead- ing an extended school will be:

- What are the school's priorities?
- What do you know about your community?
- What are the crucial, relevant national initiatives and how can they be accessed successfully?
- Are you aware of anything that might change in the medium term – population change, increasing/reducing employment opportunities, skills shortages?
- What impact on students, staff, parents and the communities are you likely to make?
- Who/what is the likely opposition?
- How can marginalized groups be won over?
- What is the likely capacity of the organization in the mid term?
- Who are the people most likely to achieve sustainability?

This list could be added to. However, the ability to ask questions like this and have the courage and determination to find the answers reflect the strengths and qualities of political leadership. A successful leader of an extended school will therefore possess the ability and perception to keep track of national and indeed international initiatives and have a shrewd intuitive sense of which of these to pursue and which to leave alone. This intuition is in part built up by developing and maintaining a thorough and detailed knowledge of what works and what does not work in the local context. The extent to which this skill can be acquired by tailored training programmes is debatable, as some may argue that such a skill is an inherent part of a person's individual disposition.

The ethical sharer

For any extended school to operate effectively, there has to be, first and foremost, a culture within the organization that celebrates and promotes leadership as a shared responsibility. Few would argue with Bush and Middlewood (2005, p. 112) when they say that 'any single individual has a limited impact on outcomes but, if the leadership is distributed widely, the potential effects are multiplied'. In some organizations, such an approach would be considered admirable but impractical and the organization might still be able to operate efficiently. In an extended school, however, such an approach is vital, for without a shared sense of responsibility, no such school would be able to function effectively. The leadership qualities discussed in this chapter do not all have to come from the individual leader alone. Effective leadership teams will have complementary strengths and shrewd heads will know how to deploy them to best effect. They will in fact:

- recognize their own weaknesses and shortcomings and find those in the organization for whom they are strengths
- understand that particular situations need a level of expertise outside their own which has to be utilized and trusted – this is true delegation!
- be comfortable with the fact that leadership is a team sport and that there are many people in the organization who can complete certain tasks much more quickly and effectively than they can
- accept that extended schools present leaders with a much wider range of issues which cannot be addressed by conventional leadership models.

This last point is developed in a publication from the National College for School Leadership (NCSL) (Coleman, 2006b, p. 26):

The move to a broader role calls upon the head and other senior leaders in the school to demonstrate a broader range of skills than ever before. This can be addressed in part through the development of greater leadership capacity within the school. Identifying a specific individual to lead on this challenge is a particularly helpful strategy. Elsewhere, supporting the distribution of leadership more broadly outside the school, to the local community and other agencies, is a further valuable step in building capacity and promoting the longer-term sustainability of the support.

Charisma, drive, pace-setting, determination, etc. are fine in establishing the context within which extended schools will be recognized and accepted as powerful instruments for the promotion of teaching and learning and for securing the ECM agenda. However, any reliance on an individual or indeed a small group of individuals will not create the sustainability needed for extended schools to grow and adapt to constantly evolving and changing circumstances. The key challenge for headteachers 'is to quickly move from a position where the initial momentum and impetus for extended activity come from the head to one of a broader collective moral endeavour, in order to promote the longer-term viability of the work' (Coleman, 2006a, p. 47).

The need for staff to realize the power and significance of this major shift in thinking also requires that the school does not lose sight of what it fundamentally stands for. Extended schools will require headteachers to think differently about how they operate and what exactly their client base will be in the future. They must however never lose sight of the fact that they are there to promote clear and unequivocal truths and that when working with other agencies, they never find themselves needlessly compromising their principles for the sake of expediency. They have a duty of care to all those people who recognize the potential of the extended schools initiative to create a spirit of hope, a culture of optimism and a reservoir for justice and hope.

Conclusion

The more the concept of the Extended School is explored, the more potentially complex and challenging it becomes. Some commentators have likened the initiative to an iceberg – the early ventures being no more than the tip of the tip! However, the more a school leader embraces the idea, the more necessary it becomes to change and adapt the manner in which the organization works and to re-examine its fundamental aims and objectives. Research carried out by the UK's NCSL (Coleman, 2006a, p. 47) emphasized the need for change:

> The development of the extended school saw many leaders challenge their staff to reflect on their beliefs on a range of different things. In the context of multi-agency working, though, the main challenge came through a fundamental reconsideration of what the school stood for and who it was intended to serve. By seeking to extend the degree of multi-agency working, many of

these leaders also challenged their staff to reconsider their understanding of different professional groups and agencies.

All leaders will therefore require certain qualities and skills. Key among these would be:

- excellent interpersonal and motivational skills
- the ability to motivate all members of the organization
- highly developed strategic thinking skills
- intuitive and creative thinking
- the ability to delegate imaginatively and effectively
- the confidence, courage and single-mindedness on occasions to be tough and uncompromising
- the ability and vision to be effective planners and negotiators.

And on and on! The leadership styles we have expanded on in this chapter have many similar and complementary qualities. However, at the heart of all of that has been said, here is the conviction that all those entrusted with the leadership of extended schools must demonstrate total commitment to the principle that every child deserves the best access to lifelong learning. They must possess a vision centred on the common good and present in everything they do a sense of purpose and service. Headteachers of course come in all shapes, personalities and sizes and will invariably seek out their own ways of achieving the sorts of things we have covered in this chapter. It is important to stress that whatever the flavour of the words used here – 'maverick', 'street-fighting', 'risk-taking', successful leaders come with all kinds of personalities. Our contacts have included meeting those with ebullience and overt energy, and also those with a quiet manner in terms of how they proceed – there is no single 'personality' that works; it is belief, character and behaviour that counts. They must, however, more than anything else, demonstrate an unshakeable conviction that such access as is needed will only happen if the agencies providing that experience work together to provide the right support, the appropriate level of challenge and a healthy, positive, shared culture of rigorous accountability. At the root of all that has been said, here is the need for leaders of extended schools to work collaboratively at both the strategic and operational levels with parents and carers and across multiple agencies for the well-being of all children.

Further reading

Bush, T. (2008) *Leadership and Management Development in Education*. London: Paul Chapman Publishing.

Lumby, J. with Coleman, M. (2007) *Leadership and Diversity*. London: Sage.

Points to consider

- How receptive are you to ideas which, on first reflection, appear to be too revolutionary or unworkable?
- Do you recognize aspects of your own leadership style in any of the models presented in this chapter? If not, how far do you think your own style may suit the particular demands of the extended schools initiative? Will it need to be modified?
- Does the leadership team contain the potential for some of the external services to be represented? If this is not feasible, how are they involved in strategic decisions?
- Could the structure in the school be less hierarchical? Is authority really distributed among a wide range of people who have the autonomy to take initiatives on behalf of the school?

Part 2
Working with the People

Introduction

No matter what the community or commitment to ECM and extended schooling, leaders' success will inevitably depend upon the people they work with effectively, both internal and external to the school. Chapters 4 to 8 look in detail at this.

Chapter 4 deals with staffing issues, examining new approaches to staff management and structures, the kind of roles emerging and the people filling them. Chapter 5 covers the whole issue of accountability in this complex world of people leadership and management.

The other three chapters concentrate on those people external to schools, beginning with parents in Chapter 6, as they remain central to education through their children. The other two chapters deal with the creating, developing and sustaining of effective partnerships with the whole range of people in the community who need to be involved for extended schooling to have the impact for which it has the potential. Chapter 7, where the focus is exclusively on the UK, deals with how to create partnerships, while Chapter 8 focuses on what is involved in sustaining such partnerships.

4

Staffing the extended school

This chapter considers the following questions:

- What underpinning staffing principles need to operate in extended schools?
- How can leaders of extended schools manage to recruit and retain the appropriate staff?
- What new kinds of people make up the workforce in extended schools?
- What kind of culture may develop in the organization?

Reviewing staffing principles and practice

Extended schools clearly need to be efficient, effective and successful enterprises, and such organizations rely as much as anything for their success on the quality of staff working in them. Experienced school leaders aim to ensure that all staff, regardless of age, rank or experience, feel valued, trusted, empowered, challenged and supported. Effective extended schools need to operate in such a way as to ensure that staffing policies and practices are seen as crucial to the success of any enterprise undertaken. Recruitment procedures should, for example, be fair and transparent. They need to be set up in such a way as to attract the best applicants and, as Middlewood (1997) points out, allow leaders and managers to encourage the best people to apply and then choose the best people for the most appropriate jobs or tasks. In some organizations, too much emphasis is placed on selection at the expense of recruitment. In extended schools, such pitfalls are to be avoided at all costs, since (as will be expanded on later) reaching as wide a market as possible will be of paramount importance.

Successful organizations manage to maintain the right balance between the needs of the individual and the priorities of the organization.

We are essentially dealing with a very precious resource: people. Occasionally, amid the chaos and bustle, we need to focus on this. *Fragile – handle with care* labels are cheap to buy in any post office. The usage however is priceless. (Middlewood, 1997, p. 201)

The principles of staffing in extended schools need to reflect those practices and procedures which operate at the heart of any successful enterprise. However, because of the particular demands placed on them, leaders of extended schools need to examine and revise these principles regularly and objectively in order to ensure that the particular issues and difficulties associated with staffing such schools effectively are identified and met. We now examine these issues in more detail.

Potential changes to staffing models

The purposes and operation of extended schools carry with them significant and complex staffing implications for school leaders. There is no way any school could provide an extensive and varied range of activities without being open longer, most probably seven days a week, 51 weeks a year. Obviously, staffing models that may have operated in conventional schools do not begin to meet the needs. This means that:

- many new and different types of people are needed
- new roles are required
- qualifications need to be viewed differently, as do background and experience
- new kinds of teams need to be formed
- new leadership and staffing structures are needed
- different attitudes to autonomy and responsibility may have to be developed (this is fully covered in the Chapter 5)
- different agencies/services operating within the extended school network, often on the same site, may have different staffing procedures.

The following is a simple example of a new staff role meeting a need.

Case Example 4.1

To enhance and sustain its thriving 'learning out of school hours' (LOOSH) programme, Kirkby College felt it would be beneficial to network with local partners and share physical and human resources. In partnership with Kirkby Neighbourhood Management, a former local pathfinder body, a sub group which included the local PCT, Sure Start, community and leisure centres, local sports clubs, the district council and other voluntary organizations,

continued

---

continued

was formed and constituted in order to access funding. A full-time *community development officer* was employed, devoting two days a week to finding available funding and ensuring a good media profile. A LOOSH manager was employed during holiday time to enable a year-round holiday programme to be provided. A variety of deliverers were utilized including teaching assistants, AOTs, coaches, parents and student mentors. It is important to note that the most recent exam results have been the best the College has ever had.

The additional services noted in this example inevitably involve several different agencies, all with their own staffing structures operating on the site at the same time. The task of ensuring that all the tried and tested staffing principles identified as being at the heart of effective organizations are able to operate equally effectively at the centre of all the different agencies working on the school site is complex, especially when the ultimate authority for staff in those separate agencies does not appear to rest with the school leader.

Clear leadership structures linked to secure delegation, responsibility and accountability need to operate efficiently, transparently and effectively at the centre of extended schools. Only in this way can staff know where they stand, understand how they should carry out their tasks and acknowledge and own the organization's corporate goals. Well-established support structures and mechanisms are of fundamental importance and significance, a point emphasized by Coleman (2006a, p. 26):

> [E]stablishing trust between agencies is a critical element of developing collaborative working. However, while increasing the commitment to trusting and working with partner organisations may be achieved relatively easily at an organisational level, mistrust between professionals from different organisations is often harder to address. Therefore, effective engagement and multi-agency working cannot be achieved without developing a sense of trust between individuals on a personal basis.

In order for this to happen, 'many schools have restructured their leadership teams and created new roles to meet the needs of workforce reform, Every Child Matters and the extended schools agenda' (Harris and Spillane, 2008, p. 31).

The most obvious example of a role emerging from these new structures is shown by the increasing number of school leaders who are appointing specialist extended schools services' coordinators to develop a range of extended provision. This role is often at a senior level (deputy head, vice principal, assistant head) and the coordinator (supported by a team of professionals) promotes activities, ensuring that the key objectives of the school's development plan are being met, and liaising when and where appropriate with partners, current and potential service providers and with the rest of the leadership team. Such coordinators need to be aware of the potential in the immediate and wider community to provide, for example, homework clubs, health and social-care services, family/lifelong learning, study support, local sports and arts opportunities and access to high quality ICT. Needless to say, all these activities need to be staffed!

Sometimes, a coordinator works closely with a senior member of the school leadership team. Janet, assistant head for an extended school at Sir Christopher Hatton School in Wellingborough, describes how the cluster's coordinator 'is the first point of contact for all local agencies now. They know they'll get quick action and don't have to wait for committee decisions. My role is then to see where this or that initiative fits into the extended school curriculum, and where appropriate which students are or might be affected'.

The key finding of an Ofsted (2006, p. 3) survey of extended services in England and Wales emphasized that 'strongly committed leaders and managers were key factors in successful provision. They had a clear understanding of the features of extended provision and how it would work in their contexts. They involved the whole of the senior management team, as extended services were considered integral to improving outcomes for children ... agencies worked together effectively when there was a lead co-ordinator in the setting of agreed protocols for working practices'.

It was also found that extended services were most effective when the senior leadership and management team in schools and children's centres had very clear plans, the best of which integrated extended services into the setting's overall plan, and paid attention to staffing needs.

As noted above, the headteacher, supported by the governors, can no longer necessarily be the ultimate authority when it comes to policy decisions, staffing appointments and conditions of service.

> Good teamwork between health, education, social services and other agencies, together with good capacity for leading and managing extended services, led to effective cross-sector working. The agencies were able to share information about roles and responsibilities, linked with all aspects of a child's life ... Cross sector working enabled a coherent programme of interventions and services to be developed to support children, parents and those in the wider community. (Ofsted, 2006, p. 10)

There can more than likely be a number of complementary but nonetheless independent organizations operating both on the site and in collaborative partnerships which need to be viewed by both parties as a marriage of equals, as far as possible.

> ## Case Example 4.2
>
> The experience of Wychall Primary School in Birmingham (UK) illustrates how the different personnel working on site are likely to have their own staffing structures which are centred in agencies outside the school. Wychall Primary, as well as being open 50 weeks a year providing breakfast and after-school clubs, also offers a nurture room for children, a community support nurse, counselling for families, a clinical psychologist, debt counselling and housing and tenancy support. There is also a family learning scheme where two parents took the school's own basic literacy and numeracy courses two years ago and started university in the autumn of 2007. The school has now earned itself national recognition as a winner of the extended schools team of the year award at the 4Children Childcare Stars Awards 2006.

Skills required of extended schools coordinators, responsible for the overview of all such services, may therefore need to include:

- having a clear grasp of delegated budgetary mechanisms, controls and audits
- being mindful of and knowledgeable about contractual rights, entitlement status, conditions of service, pay rates and scales
- the range of working patterns which will increase in complexity as the extended school initiative grows and diversifies.

A knowledge of the rapidly expanding programmes of summer holiday activities (driven by the ECM agenda) shows, as a sample:

- schools in Norfolk running 'science for fun' weeks and circus skills workshops
- 18 London boroughs taking part in a summer university programme which was offering 1000 courses for 8–25 year olds in classes ranging from music technology, textiles and nail design to drama
- a healthy living programme for 7–10-year-olds being run in Sheffield
- classes in Portsmouth for 14–16-year-olds in street dance, junior yoga and multi-sports events
- activities on offer in Warrington and Cheshire which included wrestling, motorcycle rides, circus skills, break dancing and urban T-shirt design.

Such an array of learning opportunities offered in the summer holidays would, certainly in the UK, even twenty years ago, have been unimaginable. Now, it would appear, it is becoming the norm. A list such as this vividly illustrates the following:

- the extent to which extended schools attract a host of 'new' teachers and learners
- that there is no way teachers can do all this on their own
- that there is also no way any single school structure could manage to run such a wide range of programmes or take on the health and safety implications
- that the workforce re-modelling to achieve all this is only in its early days in the vast majority of schools in the UK. In several other countries, traditional teacher-focused models persist and in others, a creative use of associate staff is developing but may be far short of what might be required
- that leaders who are convinced that the extended school model encourages life-long learning and who embrace the aims and philosophy of Every Child Matters need to focus hard on finding solutions to the difficult and potentially fractious matter of ensuring that all staff feel valued, motivated and empowered, whether they are employed directly by the school, are taken on to deliver out-of-hours (a soon-to-be-redundant phrase!) classes/activities or are working for another organization.

Recruiting and keeping the right staff

Given the longer hours, the increased range of services on offer and the much more open access that is provided by extended schools, the additional significant factor in terms of staffing may be the extent to which those delivering the learning will not always be teachers in the conventional sense of fully trained, fully qualified professionals. Some teachers' unions may still be advocating practice that gives teachers per se a status that allows only them to teach, the argument being that allowing other so-called non-teaching staff – for example, youth tutors, coaches, teaching assistants, students, parents – to teach is somehow debasing the art of teaching and learning and demoting teachers to the level of 'other ranks'. Even in conventional schools, such a view is increasingly being seen as old-fashioned at best and seriously misguided at worst. In extended schools, advocating and practising such a philosophy would make them unworkable. Confronting such a view and presenting powerful and well-researched arguments to support the fact that learning can take place in a rich and diverse culture where all teachers can be learners and vice versa will be a fundamental requisite for success. The TDA (2007, p. 1) reported that:

> Another consequence of the national agreement on raising standards has been a growth in support staff numbers and professionalism – representing a significant increase in the workforce who have experience, expertise and training in working with children and young people. In many cases these skills will be directly transferable following appropriate training, to the delivery of

extended services. Again, there is no requirement that services are delivered by any member of staff.

In schools in England and Wales, the number of support staff in schools has more than doubled from 1996 to 2006, while the number of teachers increased by less than ten per cent in the same period.

In this new context, the principle of ensuring that the best staff are taken on for the right reasons to carry out the most appropriate roles remains a key task for leaders and managers of extended schools. However, in light of the much broader range of tasks and expectations required of the much wider range of staff, making sure that the roles and responsibilities implicit in advertised posts are clear and precise is essential. *All* staff recruited do, for example, need to know that:

- conventional school hours will not be the norm
- flexibility with regard to contracts will be a prerequisite of most job offers
- they will, more often than not, be answerable to more than one line manager, not necessarily working for the same organization
- many of the staff working in the school will not be 'teachers' in the conventional sense of the word
- people may well be asked regularly to move out of their comfort zone and take on new roles and responsibilities
- conventional school holidays will not be the norm (this is an important change because many, especially female, staff have traditionally preferred school as a workplace precisely because school hours and holidays facilitated childcare arrangements for their families)
- the staffroom will be made up of people from all walks of life and backgrounds
- staffing practice and expectation will be influenced by all stakeholders operating on the site
- many teaching groups will be made up of students of widely varying backgrounds
- all staff will be called upon to teach a variety of learners of all ages and abilities – sometimes at the same time!

Although recruitment over the last decade has often presented major difficulties to school leaders – in particular, the inability to find teachers of the right calibre to teach certain subjects, most notably mathematics, technology, science and foreign languages – at least the central objective was clear. If you needed a French teacher, for example, you advertised for a French teacher and with some luck, patience and perseverance (and increasing ingenuity), you eventually appointed a suitable candidate. In extended schools, recruitment becomes much more complex. It may be the case that you are looking to appoint someone to replace a colleague who had developed a unique role in school. She may well have worked unconventional hours and taught a variety of classes to students of all ages. She may well have very specific skills and expertise which have made her very valuable to the school, extremely difficult to replace and very marketable!

For example, a science teacher in a large multi-cultural comprehensive in the Midlands is an exceptionally talented biology specialist. He is also a nationally recognized authority on how to integrate ICT most effectively into the teaching of science and an expert on virtual learning environments. Part of his week is taken up in consultancy work in other schools and leading workshops at home and abroad on the integration of ICT across the curriculum.

A person with this range and depth of expertise is, by definition, very difficult to replace. He also represents exactly the sort of person that leaders of extended schools would be keen to recruit. Therefore, the need to have strategies and mechanisms in place to replace teachers who are making a unique contribution to the development of extended schools is crucial.

The challenge for leaders of extended schools therefore includes:

- trying to ensure staff that are difficult to replace are kept positive, motivated and trained
- looking consistently and constantly at imaginative and resourceful contingency strategies
- never assuming that 'like for like' replacements are the best solutions to sudden or anticipated staffing needs
- maintaining constructive links with other agencies working on site or engaged in collaborative partnerships in order to clarify, recognize and respond to staffing shortages
- trying to ensure that in all recruitment contexts, they seek maximum flexibility for any and all applicants
- keeping clear and secure organizational aims and objectives in order to identify immediate, mid- and long-term staffing needs.

While key principles of policies on recruitment and selection, induction and retention, appraisal of performance and personal and professional development remain central in broad terms, each of these areas needs to be re-examined in the light of the new personnel and the circumstances and contexts in which they will be employed. Appraisal of performance is dealt with more fully in Chapter 5, but it is worth reflecting briefly on induction and retention.

Induction and retention are seen as closely linked by Bush and Middlewood (2005, pp. 141–2), who refer to cases where poor and 'unwelcoming' induction was given as the key reason for teachers leaving their posts after a year or less. Given the complexity of, for example, a full-service extended school, one finance officer in such a place was finding that a standard induction was of limited value and her view was that not until the third year after appointment did the person begin to give true value. This concurs with advice given in 1992 by DES in the UK that probationary teachers took three years to become capable of real influence.

An induction giving the full flavour of extended school services can only be effective if it follows the recruitment principles set out earlier in this chapter and ensures that it:

- shows the unusual hours involved
- encounters the wide range of personnel concerned
- stresses the flexibility needed
- makes the inductees aware of the different sites and contexts which exist.

Similarly, retention practices which are essentially short term, such as responsive temporary promotions and additional payments ('golden handcuffs') will only work briefly. The two most significant factors in retaining key staff, according to Bush and Middlewood (2005), are:

- developing an appropriate culture
- providing high-class professional development to which, from our research in extended schools, we would add a third – developing 'home-grown' staff.

Who are the new personnel?

We have met many people during our research for this book who could not have been found in schools previously. Categorizing staff is almost impossible but in broad terms, there are:

- teachers in the conventional classroom sense
- associate staff linked with the curriculum – learning assistants, teaching assistants, IT technicians, library and resources staff, nursery nurses, special needs staff
- administrative staff such as bursars, business mangers, office and reception staff
- premises staff, catering personnel
- specialist support staff such as speech therapists, psychologists, welfare officers, school counsellors, medical staff, social workers, uniformed services liaison staff
- community workers, youth workers, youth justice workers.

The list is endless, complicated by the fact that individuals – justifiably in our view – develop their own job titles to reflect very local and contextualized tasks.

The example of three young people interviewed in a Cambridgeshire extended school network context gives a flavour of some of this. The three people, Jen, Mark and Amy, are all young, enthusiastic 'Healthy Lifestyle Mentors' for the CABMAG extended schools network, based upon the Village Colleges (Secondary) of Comberton, Bassingbourn, Melbourn and Gamlingay and covering a widespread area of rural Cambridgeshire, involving many villages and the primary schools in most of them. They do not have conventional teaching backgrounds, although two are graduates.

Jen is an endurance athlete, Mark a cyclist, and Amy a food specialist. The linking theme for ECM in CABMAG is healthy living, and the linking theme across schools, classes and activities tries to affect children's – and families' – lifestyles in those terms. Nicky, Amy's immediate predecessor at the time of our interview, was a sports development specialist.

Jen's work has been in many primary schools in the network, developing school walks, ranging from simply walking at lunchtime to more adventurous ones, and setting up and developing running clubs, taking place both before and after school. We visited one particular primary school where parents and governors are also becoming involved, and were very keen to do more 'walking to school' days, for example.

Mark's enthusiasm for cycling is also having effect in his schools' area with, again, parents sometimes being encouraged to cycle with their children.

Both run activities in the school holidays and developments such as occasional 'walking buses' and 'cycling to school' days have emerged. Amy is developing a 'food for life' theme, both at Comberton and in the attached primaries.

All three thoroughly enjoyed their jobs and Mark and Jen had wanted the jobs as 'something different'. All got tremendous motivation from feeling that, while pursuing something they loved doing, they were making a difference. Behind the specifics of walking and running, cycling and cooking, lies something bigger than any of these – the need to help others understand the importance of health, exercise and diet in a fulfilling life. Physical exercise is more than keeping fit and avoiding obesity. According to Carpenter (2008), there is a huge body of research which shows the clear link between exercise and mental health, yet only 3 per cent of doctors at present prescribe exercise for those with some kind of mental health problem.

Thus, it should be stressed that these people are not enthusiastic volunteers – they are highly skilled and experienced in their own specialist fields, and see what they do in this wider educational and societal context. They bring their skills to a wide range of people of this generation and the next, and are also acutely aware of, for example, the safety issues involved in walking or cycling with children on the public roads. Already, one of the benefits of their work is the number of adults keen to take over and run local running, cycling or food groups – surely one of the indicators of success. These three are also realistic. For example, they know that success cannot be assumed. One said, 'Some of the very small schools are busy fighting for their very existence, so we can't expect the heads to give us much time now'.

Another example of the new type of role is exemplified by Paul, a youth justice worker in Hailsham Community College in Sussex, in the UK. Funded by the College, his role was initially to support its own students, but it 'was then expanded and developed to support specifically identified vulnerable young people in the town's (four) feeder primary schools ... Since then I have developed many group programmes in conjunction with the young people I work with, teachers and various agencies including Community Sports Development and the youth service' (Rogers, 2008, p. 11). Paul explains that this is the job for him because 'I know I can't change the world but if I have only helped to turn one person around, then – hey – it's been worthwhile!' (ibid.).

Learning mentors, school counsellors, instructors and many others that we met nearly all conveyed something of this passion and realization that their contribution, however small, was making a difference and that made the job worthwhile even when it was exhausting and sometimes frustrating.

What kind of culture may develop?

Kotter (1995) identified engaging and enabling the whole organization as one of the fundamental drivers of real change. Staff need to feel comfortable working in a culture where there are high levels of expectations and significant levels of autonomy, in order for the required enthusiasm and understanding to be developed. This culture will involve:

- being willing to experiment
- seeing changes to contractual obligations as opportunities rather than threats
- accepting that the job they took on at the start may bear little or no relation to the roles and responsibilities engaged in later.

The staffroom can be seen as an embodiment of school culture. Already, some recently built schools, such as Brooke Weston Technology College in Corby and Thomas Deacon Academy in Peterborough have no staffrooms at all, focusing instead on the practice of all learners being able to access facilities with smaller areas for teachers to plan lessons.

Whether this is good or bad is contentious, but certainly no effective extended school could hold on to any old-fashioned notions of being 'precious' about who uses the staffroom. A staffroom will be a place accessed by a much wider range of stakeholders and all the wall space, notice boards, bulletin screens, training rooms, break-out areas and learning resource areas will be open too.

Culture involves sharing values and an agreed sense of direction. In one sense, the central shared value and purpose is straightforward – putting the needs of the child at the centre of educational purpose and practice demands that schools enter into a constant dialogue with all relevant and potential partners.

That in turn requires that all staff understand the need to engage positively in exactly the same dialogue, a point emphasized by Coleman (2006, p. 43):

> The lack of a prescribed model for extended schools requires schools to effectively create their own reality for extended provision and work in ways which are markedly different from those that have dominated in the past. It also calls for considerable flexibility, as school leaders must quickly develop an understanding of a range of areas previously unfamiliar to them. These include the professional culture of partner agencies, closer working with community groups, parents and families, legal issues covering the provision of additional services and the wide variety of funding sources and models.

Case Example 4.3

Swanley School in Kent, England, epitomizes a richness of culture and related staffing diversity. The school serves a mainly Bangladeshi and Syllati-speaking community. The school's Youth Project runs from 7.00 to 9.00 p.m., offering organized sports, healthy eating and drug awareness workshops. The Saturday Club attracts 250 pupils of all ages and runs sports, revision and coursework completion clubs. Swanley remains open throughout the summer holidays and half-term breaks when it offers, among other things, science and literacy summer schools, curriculum programmes and study skills for parents. It also works with the local further education college to run IT and language classes alongside a network of other agencies, including local businesses and neighbouring primary schools.

The staffing implications of this not untypical extended school provision are immense. Each specialist area mentioned will have its own specific training requirements but the one important issue to be mentioned is that leaders need to find ways, through training, to keep minds focused on what everyone is there for. One example is from a large full-service complex in the Midlands (UK). The coordinator explained:

> Once a year – and we'd like to make it twice – we have a 'jamboree'. That's not its official name but as it involves over 270 staff, you can see why they call it that! Every single person linked with us is invited, and the day is entirely devoted to ECM, hearing from other groups, sharing learning and mistakes. The best check all day is when we say 'How does that ensure every child matters?' Sometimes we are not as focused in certain areas as we might be, but the day is so valuable for everyone going home having been rejuvenated in what they are doing as a contribution, however small, towards ECM.

We mentioned earlier the developing trend for schools to train and appoint what several headteachers we met referred to as 'home-grown' staff. In England and Wales, some schools have official training school status; not only in those but also in a number of others, one or more of the various new routes into teaching which involve, in effect, training 'on the job' is now operating – this includes the Graduate Teaching Programme and foundation degrees. It is becoming convenient for both school and trainee to look to appoint 'in house' the person who has grown to know and get accustomed to the school and develop their effectiveness on the spot. While this has advantages for most schools, it is particularly appropriate for extended schools because:

- in effect, it reduces the part of the induction process after appointment which can be frustrating for the school where the inductee has so much to learn initially
- it prepares the new person for the unusual nature of life in an extended school – if it is not for them, they can discover this in training
- it helps them to develop relationships with a variety of personnel which they can continue to develop seamlessly in post
- relationships and the trust involved in them is central to extended services, so this continuity is invaluable to all those receiving the service; there is not a constant adjustment in getting to know new people
- it gives them the opportunity to be confident in initiating projects for which they can plan ahead.

George Green School, a large multi-ethnic secondary school in a deprived borough of Tower Hamlets in London, Studfall Junior School in Corby, another deprived area in the Midlands, and Swiss Cottage School in London are three places (one secondary, one primary and one special school) which are all nationally recognized as very effective inclusive organizations. All are committed to the in-house development of staff and all have a large proportion of their permanent staff who came through their own in-house systems. All are very clear that an additional benefit – crucial for extended services – is that the people working there are themselves part of the community. This is particularly true of staff other than specialist teachers. As one headteacher said, 'This is a very deprived area. Most of the teachers travel to work from outside the school's area, but all the assistants, premises staff, receptionists, youth workers, counsellors, welfare staff and so on live nearby and they know and see people all the time. If there's an issue out there, we know about it very quickly!.'

Research carried out by Middlewood (2004) into a group of schools in Leicester found that 'home-grown' personnel was a common feature of their effectiveness in developing services for their clients. Beauchamp College in Leicestershire, an FSES and training school, is aware of the above points about the effectiveness of in-house training and the wastefulness of some new appointments; it therefore plans to take the process into a further area – that of administrative staff. As Jane, the College's Associate Principal for Resources, points out:

> There is equal logic in trying to train our own finance officers and reception staff through our own accredited programmes so that, if all goes well, we can appoint them straight into roles here on a permanent basis.

Such policies may well have a developing role to play in contributing to the local community's plans and services over the years. As extended schools become an ever richer source of people who not only have expertise available for the community but also knowledge of that community and its needs, so those schools will play an increasing role in the communities they serve through the relationships which have been developed.

Further reading

Bubb, S. and Earley, P. (2004) *Managing Teacher Workload*. London: Paul Chapman Publishing/Sage.

Bush, T. and Middlewood, D. (2005) *Leading and Managing People in Education*. London: Paul Chapman Publishing/Sage.

Taylor, P. (2007) *Motivating Your Team*. London: Paul Chapman Publishing/Sage.

Points to consider

- What aspects of your current staffing practices will need to be adapted and modified to respond to the extended schools agenda?
- Are you in a position to respond imaginatively to staffing personnel changes and development? Are you willing to plan for abandoning the principle of 'like for like' replacements?
- Do you have the mechanisms in place to enable all the different agencies on site or in cluster to sign up to the staffing expectations and work practices that operate in your school?
- How will you manage to keep staff motivated who may be increasingly asked to operate outside of their comfort zone and take on new roles and responsibilities?

5

Managing and evaluating performance and accountability

This chapter considers the following questions:

- What is the nature of accountability and its link with performance?
- What specific issues are involved in evaluating performance in extended schools?
- How may these be addressed for individual accountability?
- How may these be addressed for institutional accountability?

What do we mean by accountability?

Accountability is one of the 'Seven Principles of Public Life' listed in the UK's Nolan Report (Nolan, 1996). As the other principles include integrity, honesty and self-lessness, there is obviously a considerable ethical dimension to the notion of accountability, and particularly so where education through extended schooling is about influencing whole communities of people. There are clearly many kinds of accountability – personal, professional, legal, contractual, financial, professional, political, moral – but essentially accountability is part of the *responsiveness* of an organization to its environment. Scott (1999) made the distinction that responsiveness is freely arrived at, whereas accountability is imposed from outside. For example, a school may decide to market its services aggressively as part of its relations with its community, but it has no choice as to whether the community will hold it accountable for its services – it will! Within this responsiveness framework, whereby educational institutions such as extended schools offer and receive, for example, ideas for forms of provision in a community, we suggest that there are specific kinds of accountability that are particularly important:

- political – institutions supported by public funding must be subject to this
- market – the recipients of a provision need to be the major players in judgements

about its success or otherwise

- moral – the commitment to truth and honesty must be accepted by all those in the educational process
- professional – this, most importantly, may be seen as being fulfilled via a network/web of professional obligations, where the provider's focus remains firmly on the recipients of the service, rather than on the financial 'backers'.

Writers such as Glatter (2002) and Bell (1999) have pointed out that the greater the autonomy of a school, the greater the demands for accountability seem to be. While this is understandable and widely accepted, given the moral obligation of publicly funded schools to 'give an account' of their actions, there has been considerable political, public, and academic debate, since the growth of school autonomy/self-management in various countries about the actual *form* of that accountability.

Accountability and the links with performance

The demands, especially from central governments, for increased accountability in the era of school autonomy has led to a stress on narrow forms of measuring the achievement or 'success' of schools, overwhelmingly through test scores and exam results. These, when placed in league tables of schools' attainments, have led to very limited notions of what a 'successful' or a 'failing' school are. An over-reliance on testing creates a situation which has increasingly detrimental effects in several countries. 'We bred a generation of Singaporeans who were examination smart – but we killed the joy of learning' (STU, 2000, p. 1).

Power (1994) contrasted 'hard' and 'soft' forms of accountability (see Figure 5.1).

A	B
QUANTITATIVE	QUALITATIVE
SINGLE MEASURE	MULTIPLE MEASURE
EXTERNAL AGENCIES	INTERNAL AGENCIES
LONG-DISTANCE METHODS	LOCAL METHODS
LOW TRUST	HIGH TRUST
DISCIPLINE	AUTONOMY
PRIVATE EXPERTS	PUBLIC DIALOGUE

Figure 5.1 Two styles of accountability (see Power, 1996)

The damaging effects of an exclusive focus on Style A include that:

- it suggests the whole process is simplistic and measurable (sceptics suggest it is 'easier to blame' using A)
- it damages relationships at the core level of service. As Lockyer (2003, p. 308) says, '... a narrowly conceived incessant accountability leads too readily down a path of carping, antagonistic relationships between teachers and students'
- it cultivates a culture of performativity which promulgates only one view of education (for strong critiques of performativity, see Middlewood et al. (2005) and Gleeson and Husbands (2001))
- it damages the whole nature of trust between participants in the educational process
- it distorts notions of assessment, risking the curriculum becoming 'assessment-led'
- most of all, it distorts a whole view of what education is and what its purpose is.

Baroness O'Neill, the Cambridge philosopher and Principal of Newnham College, described this problem as 'the accountability tail wagging the educational dog' (O'Neill, 2006) and added, 'I'm not critical of accountability per se, only stupid forms of accountability'.

It is clear then that extended schooling, with its tentacles throughout communities, involving services provided in many varied forms and to many different clients, will require much more subtle forms of accountability. This in no way suggests diluted accountability, for 'this accountability, if it is to mean anything must have teeth' (Woods, 2005, p. 94). It is possible to compile a list of demanding criteria for any system of accountability which would give some account of whether the performance in a community was satisfactory and appropriate. Ideally, it would:

- be trusted by all those affected and therefore help to develop a culture of trust
- be open and transparent
- accept that different forms of the actual methods used would be needed in specific contexts
- offer local people the opportunity to develop their own forms specific to the context which they know best
- include a large amount of self-evaluation
- encourage the development of a 'no-blame and shared credit' culture
- be flexible enough to be regularly adapted in the context of fast-changing circumstances.

This is clearly an ambitious task but, despite the recent performativity emphasis, writers such as Bottery (2004, p. 193) argue that 'There is some evidence that richer forms of ... more extended forms of accountability might be achievable'. Bottery's argument is that education's aim, via its institutions, leaders, teachers and learners, should be to achieve a 'confident society. This would be a society capable of knowing when to trust and when to demand an audited account' (ibid.). The true purpose of extended schooling in terms of its impact upon communities is surely very close to trying to develop such a confident society, and our research into some current practice gives us the belief that this is achievable.

Issues in evaluating performance in extended schooling

The assessment of staff performance in conventional schools already has a need to show an awareness of the range of meaning of 'performance' when carried out, from principal to receptionist to bursar to premises manager. In extended schools, with the context of staffing examined in the previous chapter, the issues are more extensive and more complex.

First, there are many more personnel involved:

- not only more but different, including various kinds of employees not normally associated with conventional schools at all
- some personnel will operate off site/in outreach/at a distance
- some will have unconventional hours, working in the morning, say, then in the evening. Many will be part-time, with flexi hours
- there will be a greater age range, and job shares will be common.

Second, some personnel involved will be directly employed by agencies, businesses or public services other than the school or the education service.

Third, circumstances will constantly change. During a single academic year, for example, a community development, sometimes unforeseen, may significantly change the context within which some employee operates, rendering previously agreed targets or aims less relevant.

Fourth, some 'outcomes' in community development brought about through extended schooling will be tiny or unseen, e.g. a shift in attitudes by a group of individuals towards an initiative.

Fifth, some changes in community learning are inevitably very long term, even generational, and well beyond the span of individuals' working lives there.

Sixth, comparisons between performance in all these different contexts is almost impossible.

We see some form of appraisal or review of performance, both for an institution and for individuals, as an entitlement rather than an imposition. After all, all those in employment – and indeed those working in a voluntary capacity – have a right to know 'how they are getting on' and to have the support and feedback necessary for them to operate effectively and improve. At the same time, this review provides the accountability needed. Similarly, schools as organizations have the same rights, as do the communities in which they operate.

Questions which might enter the mind of the individual as they embark on work in this field could include:

- Who is supporting me? To whom do I turn for advice or help in certain situations?
- Who is managing me? To whom am I responsible?
- How will my developmental needs be met?
- Who will give me feedback on my progress?
- Who will advise me about my future job or career prospects?

Questions for those leading the extended schools might include:

- How will we know if we are doing a good job or not?
- How can we improve in areas where we are not currently effective?
- What if we disagree with what external authorities say about our achievements?
- How do we make decisions about leadership development?
- To whom can we turn for help and advice about the future, as well as in difficult situations?
- To whom are we accountable?

In the next two sections, we try to suggest how some of these questions may be answered. In carrying out our research and visiting many schools and communities at different stages of development, attempts had been made to address them. Some were hugely successful, some people admitted their failures and some had 'not got round' to doing anything about some of them! It is not however an issue that should be avoided, and preferably should be thought about as early as possible.

Ways of addressing individual accountability issues

Although the leading and managing of extended services involves allowing key personnel considerable autonomy, there is still a need to be able to assess how effectively they have performed, for 'a prerequisite of improvement must be some evaluation of previous performance' (Kelly, 1987, p. 215). A few of the principals or headteachers we encountered in our research for this book were surprisingly vague in this area. While they were totally supportive of a proper performance review for what we may term mainstream school staff, they tended to be more evasive when questioned about how individuals working off site, in Children's Centres, in Learning Centres, or launching new initiatives in the community were reviewed. Some simply said:

'You appoint good people and let them get on with it.'
or 'You have to trust people, don't you?'
or 'The kind of work they do can't really be addressed in any conventional way.'

When pressed as to what might happen should things go awry, these heads fell back on a personal philosophy, such as:

'I would share the blame.'
or 'I think we would spot things going wrong before it got so bad.'

This approach, however understandable, seems to us highly dangerous in terms of both the leader with overall responsibility, and the various stakeholders whose situations and careers may be unfairly threatened by the underperformance of a member of staff. While trust and the giving of autonomy are key elements of effective leadership, so also is the recognition that employees are *entitled* to have feedback on 'how they are doing'. This entitlement for every employee should include receiving:

- clarity about the purpose of the job/task
- guidance and support when needed
- regular feedback on progress
- advice about future development.

In reviewing the individual's performance in the wide-ranging field of extended services, there is a need to move from 'professional accountability' to 'democratic accountability'. Timperley and Robinson (1998, p. 164) insisted that 'the tension between democratic control and professionalism should not be resolved by ignoring accountability to legitimate democratic authorities'. They call the involvement of various stakeholders in education 'communitarian democracy', and their research in New Zealand showed that school principals were not prepared at that time to review performance in that context. As Middlewood and Cardno (2001, p. 9) argued, schools in various countries would need help in grappling with the complexities of the demands of communitarian democratic accountability, along with the demands of staff for assurance that their performance would be reviewed 'in a climate of confidentiality and trust'.

Community schooling, extended schooling and implementing the ECM agenda have moved this whole debate into another arena, and the twenty-first century emphasis on learning schools has enabled school leaders to reconfigure conventional models of performance review or appraisal. If teachers (and this is interpreted here as *all* personnel involved in developing others' and their own learning) are viewed more as leaders of learning rather than managers of teaching, then there are elements in some of the models being used by extended school leaders which we can draw out and then illustrate. These elements include:

- basing the whole approach on a 'mutual trust'

- the extensive use of qualitative data as much as and probably more than quantitative data (see Figure 5.1 earlier)
- the use of feedback from a wide range of relevant stakeholders
- an emphasis on the performance of *teams* rather than individuals.

If models of performance review involving these elements can develop and be seen to be effective, not only would they encourage individual, team and organizational learning through the feedback generated, but they 'would be demonstrating to those outside that the school is robust as well as reflective, and can submit readily to scrutiny from external frameworks' (Middlewood et al., 2005, p. 13).

Ensuring that trust underpins the process

Trust is always the basis of effective professional relationships and moral and ethical issues are always present when one person assesses another. No matter how detailed and careful the procedures are, they 'do not guarantee accurate, ethical performance ratings' (Longenecker and Ludwig, 1995, p. 68). Even the school leaders whose approach we described above as dangerous felt that trust was at the heart of their relationships. In an insightful analysis of kinds of trust, Bottery (2004) suggests a hierarchy of which the most basic may be described as calculative trust. The second is 'role trust', which is in effect what some leaders do when they trust people to get on with the job because of who they are (teacher, community officer, etc.). 'Proactive trust' comes from people relying on the other person because their constant experience has proved their worth, and the highest form is 'identificatory trust' where, instinctively, each partner knows how the other is likely to behave or react.

Case Example 5.1

Elaine was appointed to a community primary school in 1996 as a learning assistant in the days when the school was first opening to pupils 15 minutes before official 'school time'. She then became one of a group who campaigned for a Breakfast Club, firstly helping in it and then taking responsibility for it which she retains today. She passed her mini-bus test and took children on visits and later on residentials with others. She was meanwhile gaining various NVQ qualifications and took on the job of organizing holiday activities. She is now a member of the school's team of learning mentors, speaks at parents' meetings, visits them at home, seeks sponsorship from local businesses and is part of an extended leadership team. When asked about her development, Elaine's response is 'If anything new comes up that needs doing, I'll have a go. If it requires training, I'll do the training. I love the job, the people, and the community'. Her headteacher knows he can trust her implicitly, knowing that if she were ever in doubt or difficulty, she would seek advice from him.

The use of qualitative data

There is nothing particularly new in this element, as obtaining information about growth in self-esteem, enjoyment of learning, confidence, development of understanding, and so on, have all been fairly standard practice in evaluation processes in, for example, professional development and adult learning programmes. The difference is in the emphasis – away from a reliance on test/exam scores to a recognition of the range of factors that contribute to effective learning and development. Of course, quantitative data remains an element of the review – for example, enrolment figures, numbers of 'returners and continuers', etc. – but the balance is different and it is possible for a single individual example to be worth as much as sets of figures.

Case Example 5.2

In a secondary community school in Nottinghamshire, we heard a host of stories which all pointed to evidence of developments in two areas: student behaviour and staff confidence.

(a) Four Year 10 students organized supermarket 'shopping' for two elderly local residents who were housebound. There was no staff prompting; one of the students had heard of one of the people and, with friends, arranged to call, check what was needed and do a 'shop'. They organized their own rota, so as not to interfere with GCSE work, and it included weekend visits. One of the girls had been only a 60 per cent attender but was now 87 per cent.

(b) One 17-year-old boy, referred to a Youth Tribunal for an offence, 'adopted' the elderly female victim, doing gardening and shopping for her. His own studies at school improved at the same time. Their relationship arose from the Restorative Justice process, where the offender meets the victim, organized by the Youth Offending Team based at the school. The boy had been dismayed to learn that the woman was afraid to go out following the theft in which he had been involved.

(c) A group of support staff organized a number of sessions to learn Spanish for themselves, found their own tutor and arranged to pay her privately. They wanted to holiday together and eventually take some students to Spain. Their numbers were too small for a normal adult education class and, in any case, they wanted a 'tailor-made syllabus' to fit their own precise needs. They met off site, in each other's houses.

Use of feedback from a range of stakeholders

While conventional models of performance appraisal or review in the UK, New Zealand and others, focus almost exclusively on feedback from fellow professionals, several extended schools are following the example of countries where the involvement of parents and the community is a more natural part of the context, for example in Scandinavian countries. Parental involvement is dealt with in Chapter 6, but the following example deals with another important group of stakeholders: the students themselves.

Case Example 5.3

Student lesson observation
The school concerned recognized that improvements in teaching and learning are best brought about when students are able to understand the processes and not just the outcomes.

Eighteen students were trained after school in sessions run by a trained inspector and then, over two terms, they observed lessons using inspection criteria and observation sheets based on these. The students learned to focus on the teaching and learning rather than the person doing the teaching.

There were joint sessions held with teachers later and both sides gained much from these. Gail, the person responsible for the programme, feels that the whole thing is so useful because 'students seem to concentrate on the learning elements, whereas the teachers appeared to focus more on the teaching elements'. Clearly, there is mutual accountability through this powerful form of feedback. Leithwood (2001) is among those who regard this form of review as far more rigorous than being reviewed solely by fellow professionals, a process which especially in the context of community work only raises suspicions of the professionals and lacks real accountability.

Review performance of teams rather than individuals

O'Neill (1997), Draper (2000), Dimmock (2000) and Middlewood (2001) are among those who have suggested that the appraisal of teams would have several significant advantages over the focus on the performance of individuals. Some of these advantages are:

- a likelihood of better links between organizational and employees' goals
- less division among groups of staff, especially when rewards are linked to performance
- of benefit in supporting potentially under-achieving colleagues
- fairness, because of the variety of factors contributing to the improved performance of learners
- more motivation, because of the sharing approach which encourages more openness and candour
- a greater encouragement of rigorous self-evaluation processes.

We have found examples of team performance review, operating with, for example, nursery staff, the subject department of a secondary school, and Children's Centre staff, but have chosen the following: an annual review meeting of the parental learning support team at a full-service extended school in Nottinghamshire, UK, narrated by team co-leader, Sandra. There are eight members in the team.

Case Example 5.4

This is the current structure of these meetings.

1. We all individually complete a simple 10-question role review on ourselves, how we think we did, what more we could contribute, etc.
2. Before we share these, we all look together at the hard data of the team's year – attendance on parenting courses, returners, etc. We discuss these figures, sharing our views on whether they reflect our year, whether we are pleased, disappointed, whatever. We note points made re the data.
3. We 'swap' review sheets so everyone reads what everyone has said about their own performance and make notes on each one. Then we write comments on what each person has said. Typically, most feel that others have underplayed their contribution/achievement! Where someone has put they haven't felt supported enough, this is discussed – there are arguments but the emphasis is on action, i.e. 'if X *feels* she is not supported, then that is real for her and we need to do something about it'. If there is general agreement that A has under-performed in some area, we all help A to understand how and, more importantly, we discuss why. This (i.e. Step 3) is the largest part of the meeting.
4. We then thrash out our team goals for the next year – this may include improvement on some of the figures. We check these goals to see where they fit into the overall strategic plan of the school for next year.
5. We then draft our personal goals for next year, within the team context, and follow this by sharing and checking them with at least two other people.
6. Next, we offer the chance for individuals to talk openly about their hopes and ambitions, career and life. For those that want to, there will be opportunities to discuss these in detail on an individual and confidential basis with one of the co-leaders.

continued

---

continued

7. Finally (a few minutes only!), we check how this meeting has gone and whether it needs to be changed for this time next year!'

The whole thing is carefully written up, checked by everyone for any personal confidentialities and copies go to everyone present and the School Leadership Team.

Ways of addressing institutional accountability issues

It is crucial for extended schools that the individual child remains central, so that ultimately the schools will be held accountable for how well each child achieves, in the widest sense – not just with exam passes but as citizens, members of local, national and global communities and as lifelong learners. For true responsiveness, a school, according to Robinson and Timperley (1996), needs to be:

- open to learning
- willing to debate
- able to act where warranted within the school's sphere of influence.

Leithwood (2001) points out that self-managing institutions with a consequent increased accountability should increase the voice of those who are not heard, or at least not much listened to.

Thus, one of the ways in which a full-service or extended school will assess its development in accountability will be the extent to which it has become engaged in critical dialogue with groups that are not usually part of the 'normal' context. Its leaders will show themselves open to learning and willing to listen and debate, not to be populist, but to fulfil the essential purpose of ensuring that *every* child matters. It is therefore unsurprising that many extended schools use the ECM framework, with its five outcome headings, as the structure for evaluating their development. Some of course do this more loosely than others, while some ensure that each programme offered is monitored and evaluated in the light of the framework. Evaluation is crucial for development in the future and gives clear evidence to all concerned that the organization is serious about its accountability to its clients. In all cases, it provides a clear basis for trying to ensure that the school is accountable for its provision of extended services. Within that framework, choices will need to be made by each individual school and key questions will need to be asked:

- What do we wish to evaluate?
- What baseline evidence do we have/will we need?

- How valid is the evidence collected?
- How can we use this evidence to inform future plans?

Our research for this book has found examples of practice to illustrate every one of the 30 outcomes listed in ECM (2005) – each of the five broad outcomes having six subsidiaries – but there are many examples of extended schools ensuring their accountability to its constituents in an overall professional and meaningful way. It must be noted of course that many activities significantly contribute to more than one outcome. The crucial point is that the extended school has an overall strategy and plan against which its performance can be seen.

Beauchamp College in Leicestershire, a large, full-service extended school, uses what it calls its 'wheel of fortune' (Figure 5.2) to show clearly how it believes it is progressing. This includes the public acknowledgement of things 'only just begun' or 'not yet in place', as well as those of which it is proud.

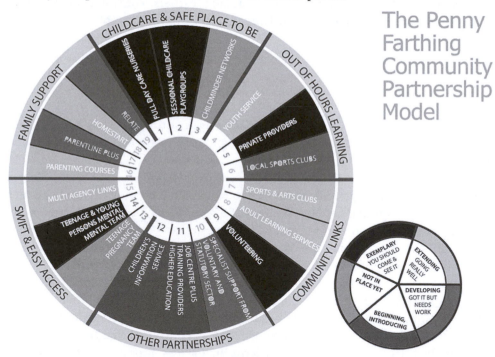

Figure 5.2 'Wheel of Fortune' Audit Toolkit © Beauchamp College

Similarly, Brian, until recently a primary headteacher in Sheffield, tells of how the arrival of ECM and Extended Schooling seemed a godsend because it was a public recognition of 'all that we'd been striving to achieve here for ten years'. He was immediately able to list activities which had been introduced and developed, and since extended school status, the school has added several more in a structured way.

'Everyone is affected by socio-economic context and those with disadvantages early on usually feel the consequences as lasting if we don't act.' Thus, the Breakfast Club (introduced in 2000 and sponsored by a high street company that makes sandwiches to order 'while you wait') not only encourages physical health and encourages a healthy lifestyle, but helps the 'ready for school' outcome under 'Enjoying and Achieving'.

The introduction of a garden has also been a great success, contributing not only to practical skills in gardening, but environmental awareness and healthy lifestyles – children are much more likely to eat what they have grown themselves! A link with the local allotments association (in an urban context) has proved mutually beneficial to the children and the adult gardeners. 'Some of the children are now urging their parents to put their names down for allotments!'

Getting feedback – the personal touch

More than one school leader made the point that to get feedback, you often have to go and look for it. One said, 'Whoever comes to the school, I try to ensure someone asks them how the experience has been. Whether it's bus drivers, builders working on site, interviewees, whatever, we need to know whether we are behaving in an acceptable way. And even if there are complaints, the fact that you have sought their opinion is hugely respected.'

A few schools use the 'mystery shopper' approach used by major supermarkets. A 'planted' visitor will go into the school, centre or any linked site, be dealt with by reception, have a look around and feed back about the way they have been treated. Any dissatisfaction can be picked up and rectified. Thus, in addition to the formal questionnaires, evaluation sheets, inspection reports, etc., there is a vital place for informal feedback on the provision of extended services where the essential focus is on relationships.

Further reading

Bottery, M. (2004) *The Challenges of Educational Leadership*. London: Paul Chapman Publishing.

Middlewood, D. and Cardno, C. (2001) *Managing Teacher Appraisal and Performance: A comparative approach*. London: RoutledgeFalmer.

Woods, P. (2005) *Democratic Leadership in Education*. London: Paul Chapman Publishing.

Points to consider

- Are *all* the staff employed in the extended school network clear about how their performance is assessed, and about the consequences of under-performance by an individual and how it would be managed?
- Have you considered encouraging teams to develop ways in which they might create their own form of performance review?
- How is feedback being obtained from various stakeholders? Do you include pupils/students in evaluating the quality of provision offered?

6

Parents and extended schools

This chapter considers the following questions:

- What is the importance of parental involvement in education?
- What are some of the recent developments in parental involvement?
- What are some possible issues for parents concerning extended schooling?
- How does extended schooling support parenting?

The importance of parental involvement in education

No matter how much a focus in extended schooling is on communities, local networks and partnerships, it is clear that as schools remain the hub of these, parents continue to be the most significant stakeholders for school leaders and managers. The use of the word 'parents' in this chapter includes all those such as step-parents, foster parents, absent parents and carers, and does not preclude grandparents and others in similar roles where they involve themselves to support a child or children.

Family structures in the home have undergone immense changes in developed countries so that, in the European Union nations, for example, only one in seven families actually consists of the traditional perception of the nuclear family of one mother, one father and two children. This means that what are often called 'significant others' can have a huge importance in the lives and upbringing of many of the children of the twenty-first century.

Parents in the broad sense as above remain the most significant stakeholders for several reasons:

- They are the first educators of children and they remain in their relationship with their children on a lifelong basis. It is no coincidence that many adults, even in middle age, remark how their parents still refer to them as their 'boy' or 'girl'! Such a relationship therefore begins before and continues long after children's links with statutory schooling. In a system truly committed to lifelong learning therefore, such people are central. 'If lifelong learning becomes an increasing reality, leaders of schools may need to reconceptualise the contribution of the statutory schooling process in a lifelong process ...' (Middlewood, 1999, pp. 111–12).

- It is widely acknowledged that parental support is one of the most significant factors in pupil achievement and progress at school. Desforges and Abonchaat's (2003) review of many studies confirmed this. Where this support is lacking in some respects or absent altogether, the child at school may be greatly hampered. Furthermore, where relationships between school and home are less than positive, even when the parents wish to give support, progress can be similarly damaged.
- In any case, for schools, though it may be simplistic to say so, parents are the providers of the children to the school – no children, no school.

While the importance of parents is internationally recognized, the practice in the management of home–school links varies considerably, often according to culture and social tradition. The OECD Report (1997) illustrated this range clearly. In Denmark, for example, the tradition of parental involvement in formal schooling is seen in *democratic* terms, not specifically educational ones. The plan there was for community cultural centres to develop as Danish society became more pluralistic, building on the tradition of the coherence of home, school and community.

This increasing pluralism and diversification of most Western societies, gaining considerable momentum in the first decade of the twenty-first century, is a significant practical factor in governments and/or regions addressing the need to foster effective home–school links with more urgency. Encouraging schools to meet the needs of parents from ethnic minority groups, often previously virtually non-existent in some countries, has been perhaps the most obvious manifestation. The Comenius Project (2003) describes work by schools in Greece, Poland and Spain which have specifically addressed such issues.

Whatever the perception, philosophy and policy and practice of schools and their leaders, it is always crucial to remember that virtually all parents have as their first priority the welfare and progress of their own individual child or children. Nothing will succeed unless they can recognize that priority within any development. Given that constant, there have been developments in recent years in a number of countries which suggest a shift in home–school relationships.

Developments in home–school relationships

In the 1980s and 1990s, there were clear links between economic competitiveness and educational standards in Asia-Pacific countries as well as the USA, the UK,

Australia and New Zealand. These led to an essentially utilitarian approach to education with an inevitable narrowing of educational objectives (see, for example, Kam and Gopinathan, 1999). In this context, parents were seen as important. 'Our future prosperity as a nation depends on how well our schools *in partnership with parents* prepare young people for work' (DfE, 1994). The OECD Report (1997) noted that the USA and the UK were furthest towards the consumerist end of a continuum of parental roles in links with schools. This 'parentocracy' (Brown, 1997, p. 394) meant that, increasingly, 'a child's education is dependent upon the wealth and wishes of parents, rather than the ability and efforts of pupils'. While Brown was referring to the UK, the USA, Australia and New Zealand, eventual disquiet and arguments for 'real learning' came not only from the UK (Gleeson and Husbands, 2001, Middlewood et al., 2005) but also from Hong Kong (Ng, 1999) and Singapore.

The shift in perceptions of the role of the parents in home–school relationships has seen a growing recognition of the need to recognize them as:

- cooperating partners in the educational enterprise
- people whose expertise is equivalent and complementary to that of professionals
- people whose family heritage is valued.
  (based on Wolfendale, 1996)

These perceptions are very different from, for example, some of the USA Head Start programmes, organized by professionals and tending 'to see children as needing to be rescued from inadequate backgrounds' (Ball, 1999, p. 201). While such 'rescue' programmes are laudable for social reasons, in educational terms, they basically enshrine the concept of the school as a superior institution with much to offer those 'below'. Later, as noted in Chapter 1, community school developments in the USA were based on a much more integrated approach, accepting that parents were a positive and essential part of the development of the whole child.

In the UK, Family Centres and later Children's Centres have been invaluable in discovering that working *with* parents rather than offering services *to* them is effective both in educational and social terms. For example, several of the case studies reported in Apps et al. (2007) described how new Centres would open and few parents would come, so home visiting, a stress on parental entitlement and a willingness to be patient so that parents could come on *their* terms were found to be the keys to success.

Of course, this kind of perception of a genuine and complementary partnership between school services and home fits perfectly with the concept of lifelong learning. After all, if learning is really a lifelong activity, it is easy to argue that statutory schooling is one intervention in that process, as the learning process continues after schooling with the home remaining – not necessarily the same home for the individual – the key place. Bull (1989, p. 117) quotes a Community Educationalist as saying, 'Ideally, you wouldn't see the join between what the family was doing on the one hand and what the school was doing on the other.'

In other words, when we talk of parental involvement, are we really clarifying:

- who is involving whom?
- on whose terms does the involvement take place?
- are the values of both parties seen as complementary or conflicting?

The context and envisaged practice of ECM and Extended Schools is able to address these key questions for leaders and managers in the field.

Case Example 6.1

We were struck by the story that Brian, a headteacher for 18 years of a primary community (now extended) school, told us of his early headship days. The school serves an urban area with residents among the 2 per cent most deprived in the country.

'Like most young heads, I felt I needed to set a good tone by supporting strong values in school behaviour. It was obviously clear that no physical intimidation or reaction would be tolerated. I had occasion to discipline Gary, a nine-year-old, who had hit another boy because he had 'pushed me' or 'picked on me'. Gary's father rejected my disciplinary action, saying he had always taught his son to 'hit someone back if they hit you'. I decided to visit the home – not without some trepidation! – and argue my case.

After a hostile beginning, it was more amicable but also clear that Gary's father could not accept my stance, as 'This is the way I was brought up and I'm bringing Gary up the same. That's the way we do things in this house'. I asked the father, 'Who's the boss in this house?' and he replied, 'Me, of course.' 'Well,' I replied, 'I'm the boss in my school and I won't interfere with the way you run your home and you won't interfere with what I believe in at my school.'

It was both a language and a stance that the father understood and Gary was ordered to behave at school as required by the head – and he did. I reflected afterwards that as a naive young teacher, I would have been tempted to lecture him on why I was right – which I passionately believe I am. This was no child-beating issue but one of the 'clip round the ear' set of values. I believed that gradually school values of that kind that I wanted would develop and that Gary as a father – and all those like him – might take those values with him to home, work and neighbourhood. I knew it might take many years.'

Judging by the success of the school, its status now in the local community and the children's behaviour in the school, Brian's belief seems to have been justified.

The courage and diplomacy of the headteacher here seems to illustrate the way in which it is possible to recognize some common ground in the values of home and school, however much at odds they might appear to be.

Possible issues for parents in extended schools

While leaders and managers of extended schools need to have a view of parental involvement and support which tries to approach the home–school partnership with the right attitudes as described above, they need to be aware of certain issues that are likely to exist. These may be of a practical and/or philosophical nature.

First, for a number of parents, there can be the whole issue of the balance of the duty and wish to provide care for young children. This often depends on the culture and accepted practice of countries. In countries such as France and several East European countries, it is the norm for very young children to be left in nurseries/kindergartens from an early age while parents work. In the UK, the post-feminist debate about mothers working and/or caring for children means that some parents, especially mothers, can feel guilt about their children being looked after by formal carers, even when government policies encourage them to return to paid employment. Some Oxford University research found that spending long hours in nurseries – more than 35 hours a week – caused anxiety to some children (Sylva et al., 2004), and other research showed that UK parents spent less time with their children than other parents in Europe. Economic imperatives meant that most families had to and wanted to consider childcare, but it did not necessarily lead to parents believing that they should be the ones providing 'wraparound care'. Cummings (2008, p. 2) comments on how media reports can play on parents' guilt but that they fail to acknowledge how childcare is in fact an integral aspect of extended school provision. Some parents therefore are anxious about their own children's welfare but feel helpless in the face of social pressures beyond their control. Different ideologies about children's upbringing are always likely to exist and, as Sikes (1997, p. 54) explores, these can change from one generation to the next: '… it is difficult to know what is ideology and what is really in the best interests of the child'.

Many parents, mostly those whose experience of formal schooling was one of failure and unfulfilment, can be suspicious of and even hostile to schools as institutions. Middlewood et al. (2005, p. 163) give several parental quotations to illustrate this, for example, 'Like the police, social services, hospitals, they are places you only visit when you are forced to. They complain a good deal and ask you to fill in lots of forms'. As this quote makes clear, some parents are suspicious not just of schools but also of other 'official' bodies, such as the police and social services.

In recognizing this attitude, there is an argument for schools to ensure that they become ever more welcoming places (e.g. Piper, 2006), but it would be naive to think that this is as significant as a shift in attitudes. Indeed, our research visits found more than one headteacher of a school in a deprived area who believed that buildings and furnishings could be *too* smart so that they would deter the very parents they needed to attract by being too 'posh'. Mendez (2005, p. 48), while acknowledging that 'live plants and a constant pot of fresh coffee' can help, felt the success in attracting New York parents was 'largely the result of a carefully maintained positive attitude and a clever mix of formal and informal structures'.

In the UK, with Children's Centres, Community Centres and other venues, it is clearly becoming easier to provide places for parents to meet and be met other than at the mainstream school itself.

Another linked issue to be managed so that parents can be reassured is that of confidentiality. With an integrated services approach, parents may feel that something said in confidence to an individual support worker will automatically become known to all other personnel in all the other services. While professionals and politicians may justifiably have lamented the inability of various support services to work effectively together, there are some parents who perhaps fear more the 'conspiracy' notion – that *all* the services may be hostile to them and their chances of finding at least one sympathetic 'friend' (e.g. social worker or teacher) may actually be reduced by integration. This can only be overcome gradually by demonstrating to these parents that integrated services do actually help them. For the professionals concerned, this process is one to be thoroughly examined and agreed upon right at the start of sharing work and information.

The lack of confidence in many of these parents in their own parenting abilities leads to a reluctance to get involved with 'official' services who they feel may pass judgement on their inadequacies. Furthermore, other inadequacies in, for example, their own levels of literacy, may become exposed through involvement.

It must also be mentioned that some schools themselves feel a reluctance to become involved in the 'social side' of children's development, believing this to be the province of the home.

In some cases, the issue of costs will occur for particular parents, with the need to strike the balance between offering charity or patronage, charging a fair price, and ensuring that the most in need are not the ones left out through the wrong pricing strategy.

Strategies for leading and managing parenting support in extended schools

Parenting Support is one of the items of the 'core offer' in the UK that is required to be in place in all extended schools by 2010. This support includes as a minimum:

- information about schooling at phase transfer stages
- information about national and local sources of advice and guidance
- parenting programmes – run with the support of other children's services
- family learning sessions – to allow children and parents to learn together.

While the first two of these, about information, are very important, and good management can ensure they occur effectively, our research has found that the most helpful and exciting leadership developments through extended schooling lie in specific provisions and approaches to supporting parents which are contextualized to their own localities and communities.

If, as described earlier, parents are increasingly being seen as active partners rather than passive recipients of what schools and other services offer, the term 'parenting support' may be seen by leaders and managers as less helpful than 'parental involvement'. However, the ideal is surely that with effective *support* being available pre-school (and even pre-natal), especially for families experiencing challenging circumstances or being at risk, then the natural progression is towards greater *involvement* in their children's learning and indeed their own. As one Extended School Coordinator from a Norwich school expressed it, 'We started out to give more support to parents. As they gained in confidence, they became more involved and therefore the school now gets more support from them. It's a mutual support issue really.'

With schools becoming 'Learning Centres' and the need for 'Learning Communities' being agreed as the ultimate aim, the 'glue' that holds the whole network of individuals and groups together is *mutual learning*. This idea that everyone is a learner needs to include parents. In their more active partnership role, parents can be drawn to empathize more with what the school is trying to achieve if they can be persuaded to see themselves as learners, just as children, pupils, students and teachers all are. Each of these has his/her specific and specialist role, but the process of learning is what they all have in common. One parent in a Centre in Bedford said of the teaching staff, 'I never thought of teachers as learners – except perhaps about their subjects – but I have realized that they needed to learn about us and about what we have in common, not so much about what makes us different. That is of course mostly the children but it's also the community we are all part of.'

In some of the programmes we have seen, this is not always made explicit but there is no doubt that mutual learning underpins effective parenting support and involvement. We have attempted to classify different types of such provision in the following section, but many extended schools do not see them as separate and offer a whole range of them at the same time.

Types of provision for parents

Offering basic practical help in parenting skills

One important point for leaders and managers to remember is that parental support needs to come in many forms. Mary Cowley, CEO of Parenting UK, the national umbrella body for those that work with parents, warns that offering everything in group-based forms is dangerous. 'For some parents, especially those who had unhappy experiences at school, group-based services can be very unattractive. Parenting support should include options, such as a drop-in service providing one-to-one advice, home-based help, web-based programmes or leaflets and DVDs. Where schools decide to offer services in-house, it is essential these are available in the evening and weekends, since large numbers of parents work during the school day' (quoted in Schools ETC, 2007).

Similarly, recruitment to support programmes may need to be individual and sensitive. 'If a school turns to a parent and says, "There's a parenting class available and you should go to it", parents will assume you're calling them a bad parent. It's a natural reaction, and if parenting is the only thing you do, and you're told you're not doing that right, if you don't have a job, for example, you feel very undermined. So the parenting training happens in more informal ways; the parents are encouraged to come in after school and be with their children when they play and do arts and crafts. They might sit in the room after the breakfast club and talk about their concerns. And then you can mention that other parents have the same problems and that maybe it would be sensible to explore it together in groups' (Stevens, 2007, p. 12).

At the Queens Park Neighbourhood Centre in a deprived part of Bedford, parents meet to learn some basic skills in childcare and we saw a class learning to cook dishes for their families, with children present. This Centre, like virtually all the others we saw, is in a building that is quite separate physically from the school, although it's very close. The head of Centre and the school head were both clear that parents did not want to feel the school was teaching them and they should see that it was run separately from the school, so that the parents could feel ownership in a way not possible in a school.

Targeting specific disadvantaged parent groups

• **Isolated parents**. Parents or groups of parents can be disadvantaged through a whole variety of factors such as poverty, isolation, being part of a minority group, personal characteristics, etc. Norham Community Technology College developed a parental support group, facilitated by the school's learning mentors, and parents within the group have developed strong friendships to the extent that the group 'have offered hands-on support when members have moved house, needed babysitting, needed pets to be taken to the vet, etc. There is even the case of one parent acting in the capacity of birthing partner for another pregnant group member who had no friends or family in the area' (Barton, 2008). While this is a splendid example of the beginnings of 'community transformation', its roots lay in a parental support group initiated by school staff who initially identified through group discussion the issue of the difficulties which many of them had in communicating with their teenage children.

- **Minority groups** – often ethnic minorities. Morpeth School in Tower Hamlets, London, has developed work specifically for local Somali mothers for whom English is a second language. These mothers, using the school's specialism in Arts, have made various textile goods and developed skills such as lace-making. The goods are sold locally, which of course develops both language skills and business knowledge.

Helping parents develop their employability

As they are central to the 'learn and earn' society, extended schools are ideally placed through their work with parents to develop skills in the community which will eventually contribute to its economic well-being with benefits for all local people. Doing this through adult learning classes is one obvious route, and many extended schools coordinators, like Gordon Henshaw of Firth Park College, Sheffield, feel it is crucial to offer the whole range of classes including these, just for fun, such as pottery, dancing or cooking. The 'welcoming atmosphere' is essential and having overcome self-doubt and a lack of confidence, some will proceed to certificated courses, making them more employable. The UK's figures of 17.5 million people being 'economically inactive', including stay-at-home parents, illustrates the potential in society to be tapped into.

Some schools employ specific personnel to support parents. Aylesham High School in Norfolk has family learning workers – fellow parents – to identify needs, and accredited courses have been specifically written. Where parents' own school experience has dented their confidence, a specialist mathematics teacher visits primary schools in the network offering very short sessions to small groups of parents to boost their confidence in mathematics. These take place when the children are dropped off in the morning or picked up in the afternoon – at maximum convenience for parents.

At Beauchamp College, near Leicester, an opportunity was taken utilizing the fact that many immigrant citizens who had high qualifications in their home state can be found working in much lower-level employment in England. Magda, a Polish school cleaner, had a philosophy degree and, with the College's encouragement and appropriate funding (from a European Social Fund), she now administers a team of 45 Polish people – some of them also college cleaners – who engage in English for Speakers of Other Languages, core literacy, numeracy and computer training plus first aid, health and safety and food hygiene.

At the same college, Bob Mitchell, the vice principal, has worked with the human resources departments of local employers, including health trusts, major supermarkets, the local council, and other schools, to identify their employment needs. Specially tailored programmes are now run for parents, who lack both skills and confidence after years spent at home caring for their own children.

This idea of specially tailored programmes was also developed at the 'Parent House' linked with Winter Primary Community School, in Kings Cross, London, serving an multi-ethnic community of high unemployment. Parents there often started with drop-in sessions or use of the toy library. Popular accredited classes have included preparing for training as a community interpreter or a teaching assistant, as well as self-defence and textiles and craft work.

Offering help to children where home support is virtually non-existent

Some pupils, through no fault of their own, find they have what can only be described as chaotic home lives, including the many (estimated at 175,000 in the UK alone) children and young people who act as carers for the family, helping to look after a sick or disabled family member. Patsy Hodson, assistant teacher at Hesketh Fletcher High School in Wigan, UK, developed a 'home from home' for such children. She has linked with a local housing association to acquire the use of a flat on a local estate. Some pupils go there to do homework and for an 'oasis' of calm. So successful has this been in removing some young people from being at risk and changing their outlooks on what is possible that a second flat was offered by the same association. This might be seen as the school acting *in loco parentis* for the relevant pupils, in those extreme cases where the parents are either absent or incapable of providing what is needed.

Offering support together with parents in special circumstances

Teenage pregnancies and teenage mothers are not only issues of great concern in several societies but causes of considerable anguish to the parents of the girls involved. Earlham High School in Norwich held discussions with their local health trust who were charged with reducing the high number of these pregnancies in the area. Rosemary Linley said:

> We had a large number of young people who were engaging in sexual activity and were not accessing services in the community that could help them. So it was that we developed our weekly sexual health clinic, staffed by health professionals who could provide information, advice and guidance, as well as issuing condoms, conducting pregnancy tests and prescribing contraception

... we are aware that it might be controversial and therefore took great pains to consult with parents, students and governors about the provision. We developed protocols around confidentiality, information sharing and child protection. Service level agreements with partner agencies underpinned the provision. In all it took around six months to develop the clinic. At first the funding provided through the Teenage Pregnancy Implementation Strategy was short term. However, we were able to demonstrate through our evaluations that the clinic was oversubscribed and meeting a real need. As a result our local GP practice stepped in and the clinic has been sustained through their funding. (Linley, 2008)

The idea of a Health and Sexual Advice Service was found in a number of secondary full-service extended schools, some based on school sites, some in attached Health Centres. Biddenham School in Bedford had developed a similar concept. As the head pointed out, 'If teachers were issuing condoms, there would be parental uproar, via local media and so on. The fact that health professionals do this is an excellent example of how integrated agency work in an extended school's set up actually takes pressure away from schools, all for the benefit of the students.'

Offering opportunities for parents and children to learn together

With mutual learning as the 'glue' holding all the relationships together, opportunities for parents and children to learn together are crucial, and many extended schools offer these, either on special 'Family Learning' occasions or via regular activities, such as the parents and teacher ones mentioned earlier. At Comberton Village College in Cambridgeshire, joint activities include family ICT sessions and a specific Mums' and Daughters' Personal Safety and Self-defence programme. In this widespread, rural, extended schools network, where the linking theme is based on healthy lifestyles, encouragement is given via the village primary schools for parents and their children to cycle together, to walk together, including organizing 'walk to school' days.

Offering school staff the chance to learn from parents

Adopting the premise that everyone is a teacher as well as a learner, Beauchamp College recognizes that its staff have much to learn from the parents and Angela Lancini established a parent research group to develop the voice of the parent within the College. The parent group focused initially on home–school communication and a number of ideas emanated from the group, many essentially practical and helpful to parents, such as 'identified' guides at parents' evenings, emailing of examination timetables, notes when their child is absent, deadlines for coursework and so on.

More controversially, schools in Luton and in one London Borough have tried to analyse the effective parental support that exists, for example, in typical Chinese immigrant households and some Indian ones (Chinese pupils of mixed white and Asian heritage, Irish and Indian pupils consistently achieve above the English national average). These extended schools realize they are touching on sensitive cross-ethnic issues and wanted no publicity at present, but they hope to use 'model' family support to help staff to learn, so that they can advise other parents on how such a supportive ethos may be possible.

Helping parents understand what is happening at their children's school

Schools of course have been organizing and offering open sessions, curriculum evenings, invitations to learn about new programmes, etc. for many years, but this approach, though it has value, is essentially one which gives information to parents who remain passive. Far more significant in the extended schools approach is the attitude which sees parents as learners and therefore programmes are planned accordingly.

Finally, we should not leave a chapter on parents without referring to the most traditional and widely known form of parental support – fund-raising! Whether in prosperous or deprived localities, this form of involvement remains crucial, and is very different from the anecdotal 'PTA fete and barbeques only' days. The average PTA in the UK raises about £4000 a year, but some raise in excess of a newly qualified teacher's initial salary each year. Traditional social events have been supplemented by semi-professional activities involving buying and selling, and many parents bring these skills from their occupations. Queens Park Community School in Brent, London, is enormously successful in parental involvement, but the biggest challenge for the headteacher, Mike Hulme, is still to widen the parent group so that parental involvement is 'really reflecting an accurate profile of our diverse intake', and the co-chair of the school's PTFA agrees that 'we need to bring in many more black and Asian parents, which is a challenge the PTFA and the school need to address together' (quoted in the *Guardian*, 12/02/08).

The actual extent of the formal organization of parental involvement remains an issue for all extended schools. In some small countries, such as the Seychelles, centralized arrangements can dictate that every parent whose child joins a school automatically becomes a member of that school's PTA. In countries where localities and communities are diverse and proud of their differences, the increasingly pluralist nature of communities which many schools serve means that the parent body can very rarely be seen as or treated as an entity. Extended schools are well placed to tap into this diversity, as earlier examples in this chapter have shown, but the challenge is only likely to increase, as the composition of communities becomes ever more complex.

📖 Further reading

Apps, J., Reynolds, J., Ashby, V. and Husain, F. (2007) *Family Support in Children's Centres*. London: Family and Parenting Institute.

Wolfendale, S. and Bastiani, J. (eds) (2000) *The Contribution of Parents to School Effectiveness*. London: David Fulton.

Points to consider

- Have you a space at school or nearby that could be designated as a facility for parents? If so, could they be involved in issues of facilities, decor, etc?
- What opportunities might be provided for parents and their children to learn together? Do you include learning activities where the emphasis is much more on the child teaching the parent, e.g. in mastering the latest technology?
- How representative of your parents in the community as a whole are the parents currently on your PTA or similar organization? What steps, however small, might be taken to widen this representation?

7

Creating dynamic partnerships

This chapter considers the following questions:

- What are the current challenges facing school leaders in attempting to estab-lish effective partnerships?
- What are the major obstacles that need to be overcome?
- How can all those involved create a win–win solution for the ECM agenda?
- What are the various partners' fundamental needs and expectations?

The current major challenges

In 2005, the UK Minister for Children, Young People and Families, addressing a national extended schools' conference, stressed the importance of the extended ser-vices initiative. She said: '... we are trying to create an infrastructure that will be permanent whatever political future there might be. A permanent infrastructure of seamless services for children and families, transforming the quality, the accessibil-ity and the coherence of services so that every child and young person is able to reach their full potential.'

She made it clear that the extent to which this goal is achieved will be dependent on, among other things:

- the degree to which there is close cooperation between all partners working in education, childcare, Children's Centres and children's services
- whether or not coherent, integrated and sustainable offers that can be made to children and families.

Historically, the extent to which schools have been able to form positive, mutually beneficial links with their local communities has varied enormously. Key factors which have been instrumental in whether or not schools have tended to look inwards or outwards as far as their existing and/or potential partners are concerned include:

- the real or perceived reputation of the school in and by the local community
- the extent to which the governors and senior leaders consider that they need to build such relationships
- the attitude of the head with regard to matters which may not be seen as directly and unequivocally related to the day job of running a school
- the willingness of the staff to look outside the immediate needs and challenges of the classroom, the national curriculum, examination results, etc.
- the attitude of local stakeholders to schools in particular and education in general
- the location of the school: small rural schools separated by roads, wide open spaces and with limited scope for business development or entrepreneurial successes may well be less enthusiastic about establishing 'dynamic partnerships'
- the prejudices built up over many years by those in schools and those not in schools about how genuine or effective either side is in delivering on promises, outcomes and their commitments.

The last of these perhaps reflects an entrenched attitude on both sides that has existed for perhaps the last 50 years or more. All too often, opinions as to, for instance, the effectiveness of schools, the motives and aspirations of local businesses, the efficiency of social services, the impact of the police, the altruism of potential sponsors, the bureaucracy of public bodies, etc. have been based on anecdote and rumour rather than on fact. The overall effect has been to make potential partners hesitant and dubious about possible collaborations rather than excited and upbeat about them. If the extended schools initiative is successful in breaking down these barriers and opening up constructive dialogue between all those who have a responsibility for meeting the needs of young people, then it will, in this alone, have achieved a great deal.

Identifying the obstacles, recognizing the barriers

As discussed earlier, schools, and by definition school leaders, need to recognize that they are free to develop a model of extended provision that meets their specific needs and those of their students, their parents and the communities in which they live. The extended services philosophy encourages schools to develop collaborative activities that will realize their own vision and establish inter-agency partnerships which will provide targeted support for all those with a vested interest in ECM. The

(UK) Ofsted report (2006, p. 15) on extended services made it clear what needed to be in place for partnerships to work. Success, it claimed:

> ... depended on settings (partnership contexts) *knowing what they wanted to achieve* from the provision for their whole community and how they might support its development and sustainability. Experienced settings recognised that sustainability was not just about grants, but about *maintaining interest, encouraging involvement*, and *anticipating* and *adapting* to change. Good settings understood and developed ways to include extended activities in their overall work. Excellent continuing communication ensured that participants had a say in developments and a well defined and respected role. Children, parents and other adults developed a sense of ownership of the services provided and wanted more.

The emphasis on communication, on shared understanding of the key objectives, and on working together for mutual gain, highlight the importance of all those potential partners signing up to initiatives which will not only support the individual child but will also make those individual partners more effective.

Case Example 7.1

In 2008, two headteachers of large London comprehensives were arguing against the erection of security arches in their schools to combat the rising incidence of knife crime. They wanted instead to work with the community to try to create an ethos where the kids did not want knives in school. They wanted their students to feel protected in school and see it as a haven from what happens on the estates and where children and young people come to adults and trust them to deal with it. As a response, the Association of Chief Police Officers detailed plans to 'nip youth offending in the bud' through Safer School Partnerships. Police plan to work with schools and other community groups to target prolific young offenders who are involved with guns or knives.

This example seems to exemplify the importance of agencies working together towards a common goal. In this instance, all the parties came together in order to find a long-term solution rather than a quick reactionary fix to the problem. It was in the schools' best interest to find a way of changing the attitudes and misguided aspirations of the minority of their students who were intent on espousing and practising violence and intimidation. It was clearly a far more sensible approach by the police to put forward imaginative and proactive proposals to help support the schools in changing the culture. Equally clear was the need for the local community to support both parties in addressing and solving this deep-seated and apparently insoluble problem.

Traditionally, the lack of collaboration between agencies charged with the responsibility of delivering the ECM agenda has centred on a number of fundamental difficulties when it comes to these sometimes seemingly quite separate organizations working together effectively. We have already mentioned the suspicion and prejudice (on all sides) which has tended to cloud judgements and confirm inaccurate rumours about each organization's goals and practices. A headteacher interviewed by Cummings et al. (2005, p. 35) drew attention to agencies' different priorities:

> One of the key things is that we can presume in Education that other services have got the same priorities which is not the case at all and, as for Social Services, their priority is very much in terms of children at risk and accidental injury. And I think one of the key things is trying to create multi-disciplinary teams where the focus is on outcomes and not service representation.

All the time people working in specific services are ignorant about what is going on in other related agencies, so there is much less likelihood that there will be a genuine commitment from anyone to share information, benefit from each other's expertise or recognize how much more targeted and effective these disparate efforts would be if they were channelled more directly and corporately at the needs of the child.

Jan Trigg, an area manager of Home-Start, an organization set up in Leicester (UK) in 1973 to use volunteers to provide support, friendship and practical help to parents at home (there are now 345 Home-Start centres across the UK), expressed a great deal of frustration when she said about a lack of response from some schools:

> We recruit our trainers from the local community and work with parents who have frequently not had good experiences at and of school. They lack the parenting skills to prepare their own children from starting at school in a positive frame of mind and all too often, these children fail to reach anything like their potential. Targeting as we do the 2–5 year olds means that we are in a strong position to offer schools constructive advice on how best to manage these children and get the best out of them and their families. Too often, however, we find that there is no genuine desire on the part of schools, extended or otherwise, to work with us or take advantage of the fact that we really know these families and have established a great working relationship with them. It is such a waste!

> ## Case Example 7.2
>
> Jo and her husband Carl had a son of 6 and daughter of 2 when they were referred to Home-Start by Jo's health visitor. Jo was suffering from depression following many years of mental health problems. Their son Mark was displaying serious behavioural issues. Carl's job took him away from home and their extended family lived in Liverpool and the West Midlands respectively. While Jo's parents were supportive, living 50 miles away, working full time and having their own health issues made this support limited. Carl's family were critical and unsupportive. Carl had three teenage children from a previous marriage who came to stay during school holidays, adding to the family pressures.
>
> Jo had very negative memories of her school days where she was frequently bullied and enjoyed far from positive relationships with the majority of staff. A volunteer was placed with Jo to support the work of the mental health professionals and to begin to build her self-esteem and self-confidence. The volunteer, a retired primary school teacher, began by spending time with Jo and Jenny while Mark was at school. Jo was unable to attend parents' evenings and found it difficult to respond to written correspondence from the school. The volunteer began to accompany Jo and explained that the school was there to help Mark get through his difficulties.
>
> The volunteer made a huge difference to Jo within the home but Jo still struggled to engage outside with parents and groups. As a result, Home-Start with the support of a large, local, full-service extended school, accessed the funding for Jo to attend a parenting course. She quickly began to grow in confidence and discovered that she was able to take control of situations and manage her children much more effectively. Jo's confidence grew to the extent that she spoke at a regional conference about how she had benefited from the support. Now she speaks regularly on behalf of the scheme to new volunteers, MPs, local councillors and even attended an extended services event at the House of Commons explaining to people how the services had helped.

The significance of this example is that the positive outcomes cited only happened because Home-Start was working with a school that had a clear remit with regard to its role in delivering extended services, understood the work of this local organization and helped source the funding. Without those factors, little or nothing would have happened and the problems being experienced by this family would certainly have escalated dramatically.

One of the ironies behind all real or potential barriers to collaborative working is the fact that the vast majority of those people in these organizations will accept without question that the problems encountered by young people and their families do not come singly and that the only way to avoid crisis management or costly and ineffective duplication of efforts and resources is for all those agencies to join together for the common good. And yet, even allowing for the fact that this is acknowledged by just about everyone involved in the process of delivering the ECM agenda, there are still widespread practices and aberrations that are difficult to defend. A headteacher (Roger Tanner) of a large urban school (actually deliberately built in the 1970s in a shopping centre as a pilot extended school) expressed his frustration with social services when he said that, even though they had an office on his school campus, if he needed any advice, financial support or official sanctioning of a proposed solution to a difficult issue he was dealing with, he had to travel six miles across town to another social services office to obtain official approval of his actions.

How to create a win–win solution: seamless services

A fundamental task faced by school leaders of extended schools is to recognize and confront the major barrier expressed most commonly by members in different organizations, namely the fear that their territory is being invaded by less qualified amateurs. Cummings et al. (2005, p. 40) mention a local authority officer who complained:

> We have been in discussions with the voluntary and community sector who, we have to say, are very suspicious of extended schools and Children's Centres. They feel we are treading on their toes and are very anxious about what we are trying to do and are slightly distrustful of schools so we need to try to reassure them and support each other. Their concern is that schools will offer it all and make community centres redundant and we have to be careful not to do that. We do not want to replicate the existing services.

This level of concern highlights the issues which are getting in the way of effective collaboration, namely:

- the level and breadth of the suspicion
- the strong advocacy of territorialism that comes across in what is being said
- the real sense of parties being defensive
- the acute feeling of anxiety
- the misguided concern that one agency's success may make another agency/facility redundant – even if by doing so, the revised solution is more cost-effective and productive!

Such attitudes and approaches will inevitably result in some agencies failing to recognize that they are actually part of the solution, not separate from it.

Another major obstacle is the level of constraint imposed on certain organizations, in particular financial constraints. Even before the FSES initiative, school leaders would, for example, frequently draw attention to:

- the lack of suitably qualified educational welfare officers
- shortcomings in the educational psychology service
- insufficient available counselling support
- inadequate local targeted support for those children who are unsuitable for mainstream schooling
- far too little community policing
- inadequate specialist help with regard to sexual health/family breakdown.

Such shortcomings can be seen to be exacerbated when it comes to extended services. All too often, it appears to be the organization behind the organization that is imposing the constraints, seemingly unaware of the context in which these organizations are trying to operate or the mid/long-term disastrous consequences of failing to see the wider picture. One solution to this problem was advocated by a head of an FSES when he said: 'Go to the top not the bottom. Go to the Chief Executives and the Directors and then you will have a strategy. Doing this is a big step up the ladder.'

Other more cynical leaders will more likely be less optimistic that such an approach will break down the barriers and remove the constraints. They will argue that it is not necessarily the case that a chief executive will have a clear grasp of the way his or her organization operates or what the real or potential shortcomings may be.

If school leaders are going to enjoy any significant levels of success in overcoming these obstacles, tied in as they are with the complexity that surrounds effective partnership working, they will need to break down these barriers in order that the FSES model can impact successfully and effectively in delivering targeted and appropriate levels of support to young people. The following example powerfully illustrates how partners can work together effectively to utilize their respective strengths and resources to maximum effect.

Case Example 7.3

A family support and advocacy worker, employed by the Red Cross, has been based at an academy offering extended services in the Midlands (UK). She is regarded by the families she works with as someone who works in the school but is not employed by them. The fact that she has this perceived neutral status means that she engenders trust among those she is supporting. She takes referrals (a process that is managed by the Red Cross, not the school) from teachers and the special needs coordinator. She goes out into the community to make family visits and network with other voluntary support services. Issues she deals with could, for example, be to do with housing, parenting skills, debt management and domestic violence. She works closely with the school's pastoral teams and

continued

continued

with those teachers at the academy who are responsible for child protection. She orga-
nizes coffee mornings, stands at the front gate every morning and evening, and is in an ideal
position to bring agencies together in a much more targeted way to support families who
need help. She is not in any sense a social worker and, even more importantly, not viewed
as one. Her role helps to break down the barriers and reduce the sense of fear and appre-
hension about so-called conventional support services.

The fact that this particular worker was seen by the families in need as a friend
who was there to give support, rather than a potential enemy who was there to
judge and punish them for their inadequacies and shortcomings, meant that they
could be given the right sort of help much more easily and directly. The other
important point to note is that the only way this model could exist is through both
organizations working in partnership by acknowledging each other's strengths,
restrictions and areas of expertise.

A headteacher of an FSES in Solihull has been working with his metropolitan
borough council to establish collaborative working practices that actually make an
impact. He believes that there is a real need to reflect on who needs to become
involved before a situation becomes a crisis. It is important, he says, to create:

> co-ordinated and cohesive multi-agency networks which bring together a
> range of expertise and can support young people and families when they need
> this support. The value is the relationship between professionals. The culture
> in which we work is one of trust and respect for each other's role, skill and
> knowledge and one of learning from each other. There needs to be a move
> away from the 'empire building' mentality.

Case Example 7.4

A school in the UK's south-east was attempting to deal with a growing unemployment
trend in the area and an increasing tendency on the part of some of its most talented students to not apply for university. The leadership team took the decision to enter into a
number of partnerships with local businesses who had a reputation for recruitment and
training. The deal struck was that each year the school would provide up to five of its best
students to compete for one job in each/any of the businesses who had vacancies. The successful applicant(s) would then be guaranteed a one-year contract and appropriate
professional development. To date, twenty students have taken up post in a number of different occupations, including accountancy and architecture and the scheme is expanding
year on year.

Agencies working in true partnership see the clear benefits of joint planning and delivery and place a premium on the value of conversations. They identify that so much can be achieved without many additional resources and recognize that what is needed is simply a different way of delivering existing services.

Fundamental needs and expectations

This 'different way of working' carries with it a number of implications about widespread current practice and what needs to change. A number of important factors must be borne in mind if there is going to be any real likelihood of fundamental change in the way partners work together. For example:

- the statutory sector needs to learn lessons from the voluntary sector which, because of the precarious and inconsistent nature of its funding, is much more adept at recognizing and responding to the need for change
- schools are fairly responsive to local and wider community needs in the main but ineffective communication with 'outside agencies' can frequently be an issue
- joint working is very important: the worst thing you can do is have too many organizations intervening with a single family
- multi-agency working is still in its infancy in all schools, including extended schools. School leaders may need to undertake a steep learning curve in order to acquire the knowledge and skill base needed to make such collaborations work effectively
- school leaders need to value the partnerships by establishing a positive transparency about the key objectives and trust other agencies to have the wit and wisdom to provide a relevant and necessary service
- schools have to be prepared to access and share data and acknowledge that all bona-fide organizations will have data-sharing protocols designed to protect children's and families' rights
- schools need to acknowledge that they most probably know very little about what is going on in their local community or what organizations exist to help them deal with some of the really taxing problems they are facing. It is very important, for example, that they do not replicate what is already happening.

Significantly, this list places great emphasis on the need for schools to change their methods of operation.

Although it is probably true that many external agencies do not by their nature seek out schools in order to develop partnerships, it is equally true that the more enterprising, entrepreneurial and welcoming a school is in its relationships with other agencies, the more likely it is that effective collaborations will flourish.

Dynamic partnerships rarely if ever happen by chance and frequently schools will have to be single-minded (and on occasions bloody-minded) in the way they look to form links with the local and wider community. There are without doubt significant time, financial and personnel implications: school leaders have to be prepared to expend a great deal of energy and sustain high levels of commitment and determination to make sure that the partnerships they are looking to establish prosper and flourish. These are not activities for the faint- or half-hearted!

Case Example 7.5

Three schools in Bedfordshire – a lower, middle and upper school – joined forces to create a learning community. Central to their key objectives were to set corporate goals, engage in real collaborative partnerships centred as far as possible on seamless transition and take on corporate responsibility for outcomes across the community. Sited as this partnership was in an area of real deprivation, it was essential that the local community became involved as integral members of the learning alliance. In order for this to happen, a neighbourhood centre was created in a building close to the three schools but, significantly, not housed in any of them. Run by a duly appointed centre coordinator, the centre quickly established partnerships with a range of external agencies. These included, among others, the local Primary Care Trust, the Health Improvement Team, the Youth Service, Social Services, Job Centre Plus, parent and toddler groups and the Citizens' Advice Bureau. One of the initiatives that came out of this development was the creation of a Well-being Centre in the upper school which was part-run by nurses and a doctor who also worked in the Neighbourhood Centre. An additional major benefit of the scheme was the manner in which all those involved in this learning community were able to target their resources much more effectively. Parents began working proactively in their local community, the significant number of home-educated students in the community were supported rather than ostracized by their local schools and the regular meetings attended by all the relevant agencies became, in the words of the centre coordinator, 'exciting, proactive workshops rather than lifeless bureaucratic talk shops' – as they had been in the past.

This case strongly exemplifies what needs to be done in order to create dynamic partnerships that really do make an impact on the ECM agenda. What they managed to do should be seen as encapsulating guiding principles for all those school leaders who are genuinely committed to delivering extended services. Specifically, they:

- appointed staff who knew the local community intimately and recognized the potential it had for genuine growth

- were open to all and any offers of help from those people working in the community who could make a relevant and worthwhile contribution – and they did not pre-judge anyone
- looked to exploit opportunities to use local residents, young mothers, youth workers, young and not-so-young professionals with a social conscience, as well as past students, to help improve the quality and range of what they were offering and, just as important, provide the even younger members of the community with excellent role models
- put in place transparent straightforward mechanisms to allow those in need to access the relevant services and support networks
- maintained a high but nonetheless rational degree of optimism about what could be achieved now and in the future.

These crucial points were well exemplified in the experience of the Hatton Partnership in Wellingborough, Northamptonshire, a town with identified deprived areas. As a first move into the field, they appointed Vanessa as a coordinator, someone with a background not in teaching but in youth, volunteering and community work. Her first step was to work with the Sir Christopher Hatton School (secondary) to get a room identified as a parents' room, to be used in an informal way by parents as and when they needed it.

Then, without any real strategic plan, but with a vision of the partnership school heads of what might ultimately be possible, and following an audit across the schools involved, facilities and services/activities began to be offered to all kinds of groups and taken up by various users:

- breakfast and luncheon clubs
- after-school care for infants and young people
- pre-school playgroups, parent and toddler groups
- youth clubs
- interfaith groups, holiday playcare, friendship clubs.

This included some of these being based in link primary schools, a Children's Centre in the middle of a local housing estate, and the Victoria Centre.

Although the external agencies do not yet see all these as one unit, already many local needs are being met through this thriving programme. These community needs having been demonstrated, strategic decisions and planning were able to be taken, the leaders now knowing that these would not be theoretical but were able to build on what was there. 'Sometimes,' as Vanessa said, 'you just have to go for it!'

The UK's Ofsted report (2008, p. 15) evaluating the impact of children's centres and extended schools echoed some of the above practice. It found that:

schools that provided the most effective services integrated these within their planning for whole school improvement, because they were clear about the overall outcomes they wished to achieve for their pupils. There was also some evidence of schools radically rethinking their ways of working to provide better access to services. In particular, these schools had set up teams of staff from different professional backgrounds to support vulnerable pupils. This enabled swift action to be taken, preventing difficulties becoming more serious.

Here again, the emphasis is very much on schools being innovatively proactive in the way in which they reach out to their local and wider community. Although there is clearly a rational argument for other agencies to become involved in this way, it still needs clear, firm and enlightened leadership from schools to make it happen. The report cites one school (unnamed) which illustrated how schools will need to operate now and in the future.

Case Example 7.6

An extended services centre on the site of a specialist school focused on integrated family support, multi-agency planning and rapid response, and support for behaviour and transition. The centre accommodated a few organizations, but it was also used effectively for training and drop-in work. The multi-agency, school-based team included staff supporting pupils with learning difficulties and disabilities and behaviour problems, as well as an educational psychologist, home/school support workers and a family therapist. The team had made very good progress, evidenced by speedier referrals, earlier interventions, improved record-keeping and the way in which the school's team acted as a conduit to keep families informed.

Two of the general weaknesses identified in the report were the lack of efficiency and effectiveness of monitoring and evaluation. If leaders of extended schools are to maintain a high-quality network of dynamic partnerships, it is essential that they keep up to date with what is happening on the ground, have mechanisms to identify needs and emerging weaknesses and ensure that high standards of delivery are sustained. Passion is no guarantee of quality! It was suggested that the schools in areas of greatest deprivation often showed a passionate commitment to meeting pupils' needs, but did not always focus on standards of achievement. A small minority of schools had not realized the potential of activities and other services to raise achievement, including for the most able.

It is therefore important that schools have formal and informal mechanisms in place for monitoring and evaluating the quality of service that is being provided. In this way, they will be able to track the progress (and regress) of individuals and groups, react quickly to aspects of their work which is failing to meet expectations and plan future developments based on the real as well as the perceived needs of the local and wider community.

Much of this chapter has considered the challenges facing school leaders as they reach out into the local and wider community. What has emerged is the extent to which schools will have to be proactive, innovative and courageous in breaking the conventional mode of how schools operate. What is equally clear are the great benefits to be had – for the child, school and community – if they get it right.

Further reading

Cheminais, R. (2007) *Extended Schools and Children's Centres*. London: Routledge.
Hill, R. (2007) *Achieving More Together: Adding value through partnerships*. London: Esmee Fairbairn Foundation.
Lumby, J. and Foskett, N. (eds) (1999) *Managing External Relations in Schools and Colleges*. London: Paul Chapman Publishing.

Points to consider

- Brian Taylor, head for 16 years of a primary school in an area of considerable deprivation in the north of England, made the point that effective working partnerships are about what he as a school leader can give, not what he can get. He also observed that it was not his job to do anything; his job was to make sure that everything was done well. These two observations lie at the centre of what is needed for partnerships to work effectively. Can you reflect on your own practices to see the extent to which they may apply there?

- As a leader, you will bear in mind that schools are going to build powerful partnerships that will really produce collaborations that work, so it is essential that they link with those individuals and organizations that can make a difference. Often, securing the support of these key players will involve some sort of sacrifice, but such sacrifices will have to be made for the sake of the common good. Who are the key players in your community? What sacrifices might be necessary to get them in partnership?

- Working with a range of partners means having the knowledge and the perception to appreciate the particular methods of operating and responding sensitively to the different cultures that lie at the centre of real and potential stakeholders. Are there particular partners or potential partners in your

continued

continued

community who may require special sensitivity in drawing them in to work with the school?

- 'Trust is vital and so is patience. If it takes time to build collaboration between schools and deliver results it is hardly surprising the same applies to developing trust and agreeing working practices with agencies and organisations outside schools' (Hill, 2008, p. 13). Are you confident that sufficient trust exists to make your partnerships work? If not, what might be done to improve the levels of mutual trust?

8

Sustaining effective partnerships in extended services

> - This chapter considers the following questions:
>
> - What is the rationale for effective partnerships?
> - What different kinds of partnerships are possible?
> - What helps to sustain them and what are the barriers to their effectiveness?
> - When do multi-agency work and integrated services operate effectively?
> - What is the key role of professional leaders in developing partnerships?

Introduction

Having explored working with key partners in extended schools in the two previous chapters, this chapter attempts to draw out some principles for leaders and managers which are likely to help sustain and develop such partnerships.

Those working in extended schooling need to see collaboration as the primary building block as they attempt to address the complex needs of the wide range of those they support, whether students, parents, carers or members of the local community. Experience suggests that if successful partnerships are to be achieved, it is perhaps best to learn from others but develop one's own style of working.

As stressed earlier, organizations cannot operate in isolation if they are to address the many complex social issues that exist in today's society, which is very much a networking one. In discussing the development of educational leaders worldwide, Bush (2008, p. 48) draws attention to the importance of networking as an aspect of this in today's context. Joint working arrangements, forums and other forms of collaboration have all emerged as ways in which organizations see themselves as being able to thrive, sometimes indeed even to exist, in this environment. The isolated school is no longer an option.

Partnerships and collaboration developed in extended services specifically in the UK during the initial piloting, when funding was available for innovation and expansion of the core offer underpinned by Every Child Matters, but, as indicated in Chapter 1, the idea that schools could exist in isolation became increasingly seen as impractical on a worldwide basis. Not only in developed countries, but in African nations, Harber (1989, p. 126) was clear that 'schools are inextricably linked to the surrounding society'. Before examining the types of partnerships most relevant to extended schools, we need to consider the underlying rationale and philosophy that should be reflected in them.

Some underlying rationales

The child should be central

Extended schooling is essentially about inclusion and as such requires the voices of children, young people, parents, professionals, volunteers and community participants of all kinds, to be heard in a way which can lead to action. Todd (2007, p. 13) asserts that 'Education cannot be inclusive without collaborating with children and parents in ways that enable their perspectives to influence the development of schools and systems. Partnership is central to inclusion'. In a telling phrase, Todd reminds us that the child – 'the often absent special guest' – needs to be central to any form of collaboration. This notion may perhaps be seen as the ultimate criterion for the effectiveness or otherwise of all forms of collaboration in this field, i.e. whether the child or his/her voice is actually present or not, any collaborative function should be aware of their needs/wishes/requests. Just as effective businesses or commercial services see the client/customer as always central, so too is the child in extended service partnership collaboration.

The partnerships must be 'real'

The concept of partnership has existed for a long time with regard to schools but most often it can be seen to have operated on a compensation model. Bastiani (1987) described this as based on deficit models of family life with the need to make less successful families more like the most successful families, with 'success' being defined by educational professionals. Developing models, such as those of Middlewood (1999, p. 123) and Todd (2007, p. 81), were based on a recognition of the non-professional or 'lay' partners having different but equal strengths, skills and abilities to bring to the partnership. Only with this recognition and full participation comes genuine collaborative partnerships. Crozier's (2000) research in Scotland stressed that talking about 'hard-to-reach' parents was irrelevant in many cases, where it was the school that was seen by the community and parents as 'hard-to-reach'. Any failings and limitations need to be acknowledged on both sides, if a genuine partnership is to occur.

There is therefore a huge onus on extended school leaders to develop genuine partnerships and avoid the compensation or deficit model in their approach. The familiar adage in people management, 'If you have a problem with someone, remember first that you are part of the problem' becomes valuable here. If there is a problem, it lies in the situation. 'The problem is the problem' (Todd, 2007, p. 137).

This clearly means that when partnerships are in action, the focus needs to be not on problem solving but on solutions building. As Harker (2001) points out, the difference between a problem-solving meeting and a solution-building meeting is that the former spends most of its time on the past and the latter on the future.

Concepts and types of working in partnership

While partnership can be seen as a positive strategic tool to achieve various outcomes, the term itself has various dimensions. Whether you use such terms as partnership, alliance, collaboration, network, multi-disciplinary or joined-up working, it is best seen as a continuum of informal to formal links between organizations. Frost (2005) describes four levels of joint working:

- cooperation
- collaboration
- coordination
- integration/merger.

Organizations should bear in mind that the closer they work in partnership, the greater the involvement will be of the individual representative of each partner. It is therefore crucial that this representative is an appropriate one, especially at a strategic level where the agency representative must have the authority to make decisions on behalf of their organization.

Mayo (2003) offers three reasons for working in partnership, which in turn gives rise to three different models as described in Tett (2003, p. 13):

- budget
- synergy
- transformation.

The first is the most common in extended service schools as it enables the organization to bid for funding, and this is often the initial stimulus for collaboration – to obtain funds! However, the working relationships in such partnerships can often become more fragile when funding diminishes, and schools and other agencies become more concerned with their own survival. We need to remind ourselves constantly that, if extended services are to succeed, collaboration is not merely desirable, it is essential.

Snowden (2006) also identified the different types of partnership that exist. These can be grouped loosely as:

1. **Strategic alliance**. These are the forms of partnership that senior managers are likely to devote time to and prioritize. They tend to form the key decision-making groups, e.g. the development of cluster modules for the delivery of extended services, with the support of the local or regional authority. In the UK, this structure has had a major impact on the way in which schools work together. In turn, this has led to increased communication and collaboration in other policy areas, such as school improvement and healthy schools. It has also enabled the local authorities (LAs) to provide increased support for children and families through a centrally managed system.

2. **Joint venture**. These tend to be two or more organizations that work together to identify, manage, develop and deliver a programme, e.g. a school working with a family support organization to provide family learning and parental support activities/programmes. This type of partnership could be time-limited and operate while the activity is being delivered.

Case Example 8.1

Five primary schools in North Solihull are working in partnership to offer year-round childcare for children. The hub of the cluster runs a full range of extended services, including daycare and a pre-school, plus an after-school club based on its own premises. Children from the host school and four other local primaries can use the facility from 7.00 a.m. to 6.00 p.m., year round, including school holidays. The centre currently has 152 children on its register. The clubs share the use of a minibus and transport for children from other schools is included in the charges. Daycare places are charged by the hour at a rate depending on age. Nearly all the parents of the children using the clubs are able to claim back some childcare charges through tax credits.

---

3. **Supply chains**. This is a partnership created to deliver an extended service activity that could involve a lead organization that might subcontract the delivery to another organization who could be better placed to deliver and share the risk. For

example, in both Nottingham and Northamptonshire, each 'looked after' child is a member of a county-wide virtual school (led by the Corporate Parent in the role of headteacher), as well as the school they attend daily. As part of the Children and Young People's Plan (CYPP), Children's Services track their participation in Study Support activities through both school and community-based activities. A multi-agency steering group meets regularly and Study Support features strongly in meetings with young people and is recorded on Personal Education Plans (PEPs). Young people are consulted at 'Chill Out' days when a range of activities are on offer and Children's Services' managers and the Youth Service Looked After Children coordinator have budgets to pay for activities and transport. This helps achieve key performance indicators and government targets as well as improving outcomes for looked after children.

4. **Networks**. These are informal, loose, open-ended groups that provide a structure for discussion, debate, mutual support and learning. They may also include the opportunity to influence and lobby policy-makers. Networks tend to be self-selecting and individuals attend for personal gain and professional development. A key feature of networking is the opportunity for enthused people to share good practice and learn from others, e.g. through Support Networks for Extended Service Leaders and Managers. One such network, called 'Dream Team', was a group established by the extended schools coordinator in a secondary school. It was set up to provide support to extended services managers nationally, where they could meet to identify and share good practice. The team focused upon the role of extended school coordinators and leaders and provided an opportunity for 'blue sky thinking'. The team also set up links for colleagues to visit each other's schools to act as a critical friend. This was seen by the participants as a valuable form of support for staff: 'You hear how different people are tackling different problems … it really opens your eyes.' This network forum allowed schools to discuss their approach to the ECM agenda, and how others were tailoring this within their own schools.

5. **Advisory groups**. These groups are asked by a lead organization to act as a sounding board. It is an opportunity for practitioners from a broad range of interest groups and positions of responsibility to use their experience and inform the lead organization as they prepare to roll out a particular extended service strategy, such as development work in supporting vulnerable young people. The Rainer/Rathbone partnership's work aims to draw together a joint offer to school clusters/children's trusts for young people (11–16) who are at risk of exclusion from school or those already excluded. They are developing a model to support these young people and also take into account the needs of parents and carers of those who access the provision. The work is to focus on those in public care, those with complex family needs and those at most risk of substance misuse, homelessness, teenage pregnancy and involvement in criminal activity. A key element is the involvement of young people themselves. Sometimes, the school

itself can take a lead in providing the sounding board and develop a local community partnership with the widest possible membership.

Case Example 8.2

In Oadby, Leicestershire, a Stakeholders' Forum has been developed. Its purpose is to nurture a cohesive community life which reflects the multicultural and multi-faith dimensions of modern Oadby and which enables the wider community to flourish. The forum was established by a local upper school and is chaired by a vice principal. The group currently has a membership of over 20 organizations from the voluntary, community, statutory and independent sectors. All the organizations represented have a vested interest either in the school or the area of Oadby. The forum has a bank account, a constitution and is applying for charitable status. They have been successful in applying for funds which the school is precluded from bidding for. This has resulted in considerable funds being received to fund community projects which help address not only ECM but also extended service core areas in Family Learning, the community use of school facilities, multi-agency access and out-of-hours learning.

While some types of partnership can be embraced by large schools and associated agencies, they can place additional pressure on smaller schools especially. An organization's non-attendance at partnership events may not be a lack of commitment to that partnership, but more a matter of staffing logistics and capacity. This may give rise to smaller schools working in partnership to spread the workload on representative forums/meetings.

Factors in success

Successful partnerships with shared outcomes are sometimes achieved through difficult processes but experience suggests that the following may reduce stresses.

First, partners need to *agree their common aims* which will eliminate any confusion later on. This should focus attention on the project identified by the partners.

Second, processes need to be agreed by which *power* (normally held by those who control the funds) is not able to be abused, but rather the power brokers operate an equitable approach to their colleague representatives.

Third, *trust* is the next precondition of successful collaboration (see also Chapters 5 and 7). Many partnerships begin with suspicion but they focus on building trust. Two factors have generally been found to be important in developing a trusting relationship: the first is based on *formal contracts and agreements* and the second involves agreed *risk-taking*.

Fourth, there is a *membership structure*. Collaboration can bring together a group of representatives, those representing a range of organizations, or people with specific skills and knowledge. Partnerships are usually dynamic and membership may change over time as new members join and others leave.

Finally, *leadership* is clearly crucial to partnerships. A successful partnership requires a strong leader who identifies priorities, moves collaboration forward, can facilitate and empower, involve and mobilize members (see Chapter 3).

Other factors include:

- **Recognition that success breeds success**. Working together and achieving early successful outcomes will motivate and start to build trust. Publicizing those early successes is often seen as crucial.
- **Reduction of duplication**. Partners that agree to work together and pool resources will provide better value for money as well as avoid duplication of effort.
- **Regular review**. A healthy partnership is one that is smart enough to undertake a periodic health check to review its structure, its protocols, aims, targets and future directions. The reviewers of progress can include not only the partners but the service users. This may well bring about a re-focus or re-alignment of the partnership's principles, roles, responsibilities, membership and executive structures. Experience has shown that effective partnerships stay closely in touch with their target audience and evolve to address its emerging needs, as this target audience is in itself fluid.

(Based on Snowden, 2006)

Possible barriers to success in sustaining partnerships:

- **Inappropriate representation**. There is nothing more frustrating in a partnership than when one or more members are not at the appropriate level within their organization to make decisions. The solution may be to form a small executive group who could take strategic decisions or to change the membership of the group in order to move forward.
- **Lack of trust**. Years of competition have left some organizations in education and public services wary of working in partnership. Partnerships on the surface may be underpinned by a lack of trust.
- **Insufficient time.** Partnerships can only succeed if appropriate time is allocated. Achieving outcomes should not be delayed by a concern for process, which can frustrate many partners. Sometimes the pressure to achieve one's own organizational targets can reduce the time representatives spend on partnership working.
- **Attitudes to funding.** Many see sustaining partnerships as dependent on funding and especially funding to appoint a coordinator, someone who facilitates

meetings and undertakes essential administrative functions. Also, any short-term funding may create uncertainty. Partnerships should always try to plan for sustainability from the beginning. Securing funding should not necessarily focus on dividing between the partners but funding joint solutions to issues that will benefit the whole target audience. Funding can be located in either one partner's bank account or within a partnership bank account with joint signatories.

- **Changes in organization and key personnel**. Both of these can impact on the effectiveness of a partnership. If there is a change which undermines the stability of the partnership, then fragility will arise. It is essential to have contingency plans for any changes that are likely to emerge in relation to personnel and partnership structures, e.g. schools merging or changes of senior staff, by nominating alternative representation.

Integrated services, involving multi-agency work

While the stated purpose of integrated services has been clear from the outset of the extended schooling development, it is unsurprisingly proving one of the most difficult areas of progress – unsurprising because the actual personnel involved come from very different disciplines and backgrounds. The USA, Scotland and England have all encountered these problems. Each discipline has its own territories, bureaucracies and perspectives. In theory, the different skills brought by the personnel should make any multi-agency team a strong one, especially given that the team's clients have such a variety of needs. Brown and White's (2006) research in Scotland however found little evidence of different agencies forming any such team. The culture of the separate disciplines may have a profound impact on what individuals bring to an integrated team.

For social workers in particular, there may be a built-in, and completely understandable, tension in their approach. As high-profile cases such as Victoria Climbié (in 2000) helped to inform the context for integrated services and extended schooling, the pressures to prevent child abuse tragedies was always likely for social services to take precedence over the wider aim to reduce social exclusion. Therefore, if this prevention '… is the key underlying aim of multi-agency working, this is not likely in itself to have any effect on inclusive education' (Todd, 2007, p. 88). This is fairly obviously the clearest example of a deficit model or what Todd sometimes calls a 'medical' model. Within the limits – and they can be considerable – of a shortage of resources, including staff, the aim is surely to develop the concept of social workers as a positive force and not merely for 'rescuing' difficult situations. Some extended schools have tackled this by appointing their own social workers, as in Greenwich, London.

Case Example 8.3

A school in Greenwich has a strong community-centred ethos, and opens its doors to a variety of special interest groups, including parent/toddler swimming clubs and a local Scout troop. Some 250 members of the local community use the school's facilities every week. The school employs a full-time, school-based Education Social Worker, sharing her time and salary with the local feeder primary special school. A key part of her role is to advise parents about the benefits that they are entitled to and the services they can access, including Working Tax Credits, local voluntary and parent support groups, children's services and housing. She found that 48 families were not receiving benefits to which they were entitled. These families have since benefited by many thousands of pounds. The impact of their improved standard of living on their children is visible, and the school reports that the families are much happier and less stressed as a result. The creation of this post has had a significant positive impact on both attendance and parent–school relationships. From the school's point of view, the worker releases significant amounts of management time and enables teaching staff to focus on educational, rather than social issues.

Often, there is a reluctance by community members to make the effort to go to the actual institutions of the services, mainly because of associations from previous experience. We have therefore already noted the importance of off-site provision in many if not most cases. The following case example encapsulates this in a novel and effective way – the multi-agency bus!

Case Example 8.4 – The Multi-Agency Bus

Swift and easy access is being offered in a suburban area of Derby through a mobile multi-agency team facility which makes weekly visits to six schools. Derbyshire Local Authority has funded the hire of the specially adapted double-decker bus, and the appointment of a project manager and two family support workers. The project manager's role is to coordinate the work of different agencies as they tour the schools – five primaries and one secondary – while the family support workers are shared by the schools and make home and community visits.

The idea of a multi-agency bus grew out of discussion between the six schools' headteachers on how to offer joint services across their dispersed communities. Community questionnaires revealed a common need for easier access to statutory and other services.

continued

---

continued

Use of the bus has been offered to every statutory and voluntary agency and other local service providers. Police, housing, children's services, the PCT, and a counselling service are now making use of the facility. A 'menu' of services available on the bus has been distributed to parents at the schools.

The existence of a dedicated multi-agency space is helping reduce agency workload by sharing responsibilities. Problems are being identified earlier, dealt with more effectively, and in many cases it has reduced the number of agencies which needed to be involved. The fact that the venue for accessing services is close to but physically separate from the schools has helped overcome service users' inhibitions about attending sessions.

One of the key factors in any effective team development is clearly that of joint training, and examples in Gateshead in the north of England and Poole on the south-west coast indicate its value. Swift and easy access to specialist services has been greatly enhanced in Poole, Dorset, as a result of the local authority's decision to set up local multi-agency teams, with the key aim of supporting schools and providing them with quicker access to information, alongside increased awareness of services and support available locally. Recruiting a wide range of partners to these teams has been linked to training in the Common Assessment Framework (CAF), which underpins the teams' operations. The head of local service development in Poole points out that the solutions to many of the problems discussed at the fortnightly team meetings lie in other areas of the 'core offer' of extended services, and team members are now better placed to help people gain access to such services, so that early intervention can prevent difficulties escalating. In other words, the recognition of the value of what other team members offer in other disciplines is established and the child client benefits.

In Gateshead, schools are being asked to be the initial spotters and assessors of need and school-based staff are being trained accordingly. Staff from a range of agencies are being redeployed into teams around schools, which will include social care, educational welfare, behaviour support, child and adolescent mental health services (CAMHS), special educational needs coordinators (SENCO) and youth offending teams (YOTs).

These teams around the child provide a more effective response to identified need through the joint training. At the same time, the Gateshead Pathfinder Project is developing greater links with the community through voluntary groups and parents to help identify vulnerable young people who may not otherwise be identified. Training for these is also proving crucial.

The key role of professional leaders in developing relationships

In moving from a compensation or deficit model towards one of true collaboration and participation, professional leaders have a major responsibility to make this happen. Neil Wilson, head of an extended school in Manchester, believes that seeing the extended school as 'a partial replacement of the extended family which, in years gone, supported families', helps to set his role in perspective (Wilson, 2008, p. 7). After decades of others being brought to see the professional as superior – and therefore in some cases – hostile, it is not reasonable to expect the first thrust to come from those who have learned to be distrustful. What perspectives does the professional leader need to have? (See Table 8.1.)

Table 8.1 Desired assumptions of professional leaders in partnership (*Source:* Todd, 2007, p. 113).

Beliefs in/that	Shown in
• leadership as a de-centred role • change is communal • political role of clients/partners • education as a transformation process • teaching/learning is powerful • professional practice is respected • partnership for community development	• recognizing expertise in others • finding what knowledges are present and enabling these to have influence • enabling pupils to play a part in setting schools' agendas • supporting personal change for pupils and teachers • supporting a critical approach to this practice • taking a socio-cultural and social constructionist perspective

Taking such perspectives into relationships with the many and various personnel that will be involved is a key requirement – 'having faith in other people's strengths and relinquish the professional's occasional fear of being set aside. With these comes a need to develop a shared vocabulary rather than assuming the vocabulary of an elite professional group' (Whalley, 1994, p. 12).

So, can the leadership and management skills required to work in such partnerships be identified? These skills surely include diplomacy, an ability to tolerate ambiguity and uncertainty, communications and consensus problem-solving. Traditional management skills used in a hierarchical structure are inappropriate in a non-hierarchical inter-organizational setting where relationships and interpersonal attributes are crucial to team-building and overall success, all of which accords with twenty-first century thinking concerning effective leadership. It is pivotal to the success of the collaborative process that any mindset of competitiveness or innate superiority needs to be abandoned.

Williams (2002) chose skills, abilities, experience and personal characteristics that contribute to the successful management of partnerships. He organized these under four headings:

1 Building and sustaining relationships – skills of communicating, listening, understanding, empathizing and resolving conflict.
2 Managing needs through influence and negotiation – skills in influencing, bargaining, negotiation, mediation, brokerage and networking. The key 'movers and shakers' are desirable members of the partnerships.
3 Managing complexity and interdependence – skills and experience in:
   • the building of understanding of the viewpoint, constraints and cultures of organizations involved
   • specific and/or technical knowledge
   • the ability to be creative, innovative and entrepreneurial.
4 Managing roles, accountabilities and motivations – understanding the parameters and constraints of each partner, such as the roles and responsibilities between agencies, i.e. who does what and who is authorized to make decisions and who has to report back.

Principles in practice

Some of the points made to date in this chapter may appear somewhat idealistic to some leaders as they analyse their current situation of the school's community and the school's relationship with it. However, as already stated, the onus is on the leaders – and that should include leaders in the other fields also – to take the first steps. It is a fine balancing act. On the one hand, we talk of empowering others, recognizing their voice and so on; on the other, encouragement has to be given to these others for this to begin to happen.

In some cases, a moral imperative may be the impetus. Given a commitment to equality and justice, situations which demonstrate discrimination or inequality need to be challenged and awareness raised about how things can be changed. Three examples we encountered can illustrate this in different ways.

First, Shula, co-leader of extended services in a school in Luton in a deprived, multi-ethnic area, tells of an initiative, the impetus for which was a sports accident! A recently retired popular teacher, Mr R, snapped an Achilles tendon while playing badminton and had to be wheel-chaired for more than a month. Like many others, he discovered at first hand problems of access in the home, local shops, restaurants and entertainment venues, as well as on some buses and in some taxis. An impassioned talk from Mr R to some of his former pupils spurred them into action, which took on a momentum of its own. The local council was lobbied, premises were written to and then visited. The whole initiative was completely cross-age, and across ethnic divides. Shula commented, 'We almost had to rein the students in!' Bureaucracy was a potential obstacle. Official local disability groups were not happy with being sidelined, or so it seemed. Coordination was the key and the students began to see the bigger picture of disability in life. A wonderful talk to them by a blind person made them see that it was not about giving sympathy but about having the same as everyone else. The campaign had many specific successes because some small local shopkeepers didn't want to lose the students' business ('If she can't come in here, we're not shopping here!'). They therefore learned what I would call constructive dissent.

The school now operates a volunteer scheme where students can enrol for voluntary work, supporting not just the disabled but also the elderly, and also includes helping with reading in primary schools.

Second, in an extended school in an East Midlands city, feelings ran high over employment issues where a widespread perception was of new immigrant families entering the neighbourhood and taking jobs away from people already there – a not uncommon perception in many cities today with their increasingly pluralist populations. The school became aware because of playground brawls – both there and at local primary schools – between pupils who were children of the two groups, each a very disparate one. Alan, the extended services coordinator, after consulting with the school's senior team, arranged a 'Local Employment Forum' and a local councillor, two local business employers and a 'Job Centre' representative were invited along with local residents. They courageously agreed, or as Alan puts it, 'Perhaps they didn't dare not attend!', and the meeting took place at the school with the councillor chairing. Alan says, 'It was a risk and at times, some remarks were close to racist but, although there were few practical outcomes, the opportunity to paint the picture, vent feelings, see others' points of view and form a few tentative relationships was invaluable. There have been no further such meetings but I do know, through pupils, of the Polish Club having Open Evenings for other non-Polish residents once a month, which seems a significant step to me. Oh, and the playground fights ceased!' Alan went on to say that he feels the school has forged a relationship with its community and there have been more positive responses to local initiatives since that time, especially in adult classes on skills updating and preparing for employment.

Third, in a rural area in the east of England where an extended schools network covers a number of small villages, each of them some distance from the next, a mobile library had been a crucial lifeline to many villagers, especially the elderly and mothers with pre-school children. When notice was given to withdraw the library, owing to a shortage of funds, there was widespread concern and anger among the residents. Having been contacted by two or three villagers, Eileen, the extended schools coordinator at the area's secondary school, offered that school as a meeting place for residents from all the villages to meet a representative from the Library Service. Invitations were printed at the school's expense and a very well attended meeting occurred. Eileen's only other input was to chair the meeting – as a neutral. She described proceedings as 'a wonderful community occasion. The Library representative, a very senior person, was completely taken aback by the size of the audience. Instead of seeing five or six from a village, there were nearly 200 in the hall. To give the Library person credit, it was not a hostile atmosphere, just animated. Out of it came an agreement to continue the service, with users paying a small fee and a small committee was formed to work with the Service with representation from each village. The mobile library has flourished since and neither I nor anyone else here (at secondary school) plays any part except by providing a small room once a month for the committee's use. However, we have noticed that enrolments for adult classes both at the school and in village outposts have increased also.'

We can draw certain principles out from these stories; that effective relationships and partnerships can be sustained and developed when:

- leaders and managers have the confidence or courage to stand aside. In only one of those instances did the actual initiative come from the school (Alan), but in all cases, there were responses to local concerns. All three professionals here found it initially very difficult to stand aside, since their whole careers had developed along the lines of taking control, especially of tricky situations. Alan was typical: 'I was dying to join in and had to sit on my hands to avoid getting the chair's attention to make a point!' Similarly, Eileen knew clearly she was on the side of the village library users and had to work hard not to take that side during the discussion.
- sometimes simply offering a facility is sufficient. The neutral venue brought people together and gave the chance for community relationships to be made, and networks to emerge.
- perceived injustices or inequalities are challenged – all three stories show this and, equally importantly,
- people realize things can be changed – including, if necessary, through 'constructive dissent'.
- people are trusted to have the capacity to make their own case and increase their 'political awareness'. The 'bigger picture' became part of the debate in all three situations.

Popple (1995, p. 338) outlined the tension in the development of communities between the top-down approach and the bottom-up approach, describing the latter as 'a measure of the health of a democratic state'.

If extended schools are to play their part in helping to develop this 'health', the role of leaders and managers in fostering effective relationships with and within the local community is fundamental. In these relatively early days in this field, this is far from easy. In the three examples given above, it is worth noting that school pupils remained central – whether the pre-school children of the white middle-class village residents, the secondary students fighting in the playground, or the pupils understanding about disability. In all cases therefore, the people for whom the extended school leader retains responsibility – the pupils – all benefited. The local community therefore is able to gain both through any improvements now and from the pupils as adults in the future.

Further reading

Cheminais, R. (2007) *Every Child Matters: A practical guide for teachers*. London: David Fulton.

Todd, L. (2007) *Partnerships for Inclusive Education*. London: Routledge.

Points to consider

- How aware are you of the success factors and potential barriers that exist in your own context with regard to sustaining effective partnerships?
- Are there any current issues or debates current in your community which could be aired at a venue which you could provide, but refrain from leading?
- What opportunities and mechanisms are you developing to ensure that integrated services can develop and work effectively? What frustrations are you encountering? What do you consider to be your primary role in this?

Part 3
Resources and Conclusions

Introduction

One of the first questions often put by leaders when a new initiative is proposed is about the resources involved: How many? Where from? Chapter 9 tackles this issue. Encouraged by the variety of approaches to resource management we encountered, and by the ingenuity of many school leaders, we cannot accept any argument that a commitment to becoming an extended school is not possible without significant additional moneys or equipment. The evidence is the opposite. Of course, additional resources are needed and are always welcome and one thing appears clear: success brings more success and this often means more resources.

Finally, in Chapter 10, we try to draw out some lessons from the whole picture that we have drawn of extended schools. One thing is certain – the future will hold many more changes!

9

Resourcing the extended school

This chapter considers the following questions:

- How can leaders utilize/attract additional human resources?
- How can leaders manage to create a physical environment which will reflect the ethos and culture of the extended school?
- How should new and refurbished spaces be designed to meet the needs of open-all-hours learning?
- How can teaching and learning spaces be built or modified to accommodate 24/7 access?
- What opportunities are there to attract additional funding?

Additional human resources: making the most of what you have!

Much of what we have covered so far in this book has had resource implications. In considering the contribution that staff, parents, local youth/support groups, the local and wider community and relevant stakeholders can and will make to the development of extended schools, we are of course recognizing this in terms of the range and quality of resources they bring. School leaders, therefore, need to ensure that they harness all those resources as fully and consistently as possible. To do this, they need to keep up to date with what is happening in the local, regional and national contexts, recognize trends, utilize real and potential resource providers and ensure that their organization is reflecting best practice.

Over the past 15 years, there has been a rapid expansion of support staff in schools in the UK. One headteacher we interviewed of a large mixed FSES in the south-east of England told us that in the last five years, while his teacher numbers had remained fairly constant, the amount of support staff time he was deploying had risen by over 400 hours a week. This school had seen a steady growth in student numbers over that time. Significantly, that rise had been reflected in additional support staff, not more teachers – and the examination results had risen steadily year on year over that period! In the UK, the latest figures show that over the past 10 years, the number of support staff has grown from 136,500 to 305,500. This has happened at the same time as a growth in teacher numbers from 399,200 to 434,900. The rise in support staff numbers compared to the (relatively) small rise in teachers is significant. This is not simply because support staff are now doing more and more tasks that were originally (and illogically) done by teachers – for example, invigilating and administering exams, supporting students' pastoral welfare, photocopying, taking minutes, making telephone calls, collecting dinner money, etc. – it is also reflecting the fact that they are much more actively involved in teaching and learning.

In the USA, a list of duties for Kansas school support staff dates back to 1977 (Kerry and Kerry, 2003, p. 71), while in Scotland (Wilson et al., 2003) and in several European countries (Clayton, 1993), the work of such staff in schools has developed as a focus for research and training (see Bush and Middlewood, 2005, Chapter 3).

School leaders need to use both existing and potential resources effectively and intelligently. They will need to think imaginatively and innovatively and not be restricted by conventional practices and established protocols, displaying the new leadership thinking referred to in Chapter 3. One often under-utilized resource is the students themselves and in one school visited, the effective use of this resource was illustrated in a very advanced way. This school has been in the forefront of promoting student voice, where listening to the views of students and involving them increasingly in the day-to-day running of the school has made a dramatic impact on the quality of teaching and learning. The leadership of the school now uses students to:

- join the governing body as *full governors*
- observe teachers teach and *grade them*
- carry out *research assignments on teaching and learning*
- evaluate the *quality* of individual faculties
- *appoint staff*
- work with other schools and agencies in the local community, including local primary schools, regional and national charities and the Red Cross. The students react exceptionally well to the level of responsibility and trust they are given. The staff recognize and applaud their contribution. As a result, everybody gains.

Making the environment reflect FSES

The need for schools to enter into a more positive and proactive relationship with their local and wider communities is, as already stressed, a prerequisite for effective extended schools. All such schools will make sure that the 'shop window' aspect of their day-to-day operations reflects their best features. Anyone who has phoned a school and found the reception to be amateurish, unhelpful, vague and at worst plain rude knows how their view of that school is perhaps tainted forever. Equally, visiting a school where the physical reception is unwelcoming and where the ethos seems to be based on regarding anyone coming through the door as an unwelcome intrusion is an extremely negative experience. School leaders may point to tight budgets, the lack of time or more pressing calls on capital expenditure to justify why time and money has not been spent on this particular aspect of the school. However, those schools that have spent some money, more time and a great deal of thought and imagination on making their reception areas welcoming and friendly say that the difference it has made to the 'feel good' atmosphere of the organization and the relationship(s) with external agencies has been considerable. Moreover, it does not have to cost a great deal of money: fresh paint, a welcome board (with your – the visitor's – name on it!), well-presented examples of students' work, comfortable chairs, newspapers and magazines, school brochures, plants, honours boards, photographs of the school and important occasions and/or achievements, certificates on the wall, the school motto emblazoned large, etc. all make a huge difference and state unequivocally that this school is open to the local and wider community and wants to be a part of it.

This philosophy should of course be practised throughout the school. There is, for example, no good reason for schools to be dirty. We have visited relatively well-off middle-class schools in affluent areas where the standard of cleanliness is poor; equally, we have encountered poor schools in immensely deprived areas where the school has been beautifully kept and presented. In one school in Sheffield, where the buildings are in the main pre-1940s, the walls are painted in bright pleasing colours, the dining areas are spotless and all the windows are intact, in spite of the regular vandalism the school suffered from young people who had no contact with the school and generally lived some distance away. This particular headteacher frequently calls on the expertise and manpower (freely and willingly given apparently) of his parents, many of whom are in the building, painting, decorating, plumbing and electrical trades to help him keep the place up to standard *because their children deserve no less*. His site supervisor is a former student whose own children now attend the school and who is someone who is passionate about keeping the place up to scratch. Bradbury (2007, p. 9) expands on this vitally important aspect of school leadership:

Effective premises management can make a huge difference to the day-to-day business of a school. In practical terms, a swift response to repairs and maintenance issues can ensure that the impact on teaching and learning is minimised. In a broader sense, a pleasant and well cared for environment will have a constructive effect on the morale of staff and students and will help to contribute towards a positive ethos that permeates all areas of school life.

This is not just true of the people who access the school everyday. It is equally true for those other learners working in it in the evenings or at weekends or for those people from all walks of life in the local community who occasionally or regularly visit the school. School leaders who appreciate the importance of getting this right will, for example:

- regularly seek out the views of all those (e.g. postmen, refuse collectors, electricians, construction workers, visiting lecturers from higher education, local residents, councillors, etc.) who visit the school
- make sure the signposting is clear and easy to follow
- have ample car parking in place for visitors (including, of course, the disabled), again clearly signed
- ensure that any vandalism or graffiti is removed as quickly as possible and certainly within 24 hours
- have systems in place to ensure that co-users of spaces are managed well and efficiently
- maintain excellent communication links with all those accessing the site
- establish and maintain first-class booking procedures.

By observing good practice such as is listed here, it is far more likely that a school can establish much closer and mutually productive links with potential providers. Kendall et al. (2007, p. 21) quote an example of a school they visited that was reaching out to the business sector: 'At school X we set up a business centre. If you were a local business in that area, rather than send people down to £400 for a day's training, we could be much more bespoke, working with Business Link to help set up courses locally for people and we also provided self-help groups. Again that was good because the businesses contributed a lot to the school. The business centre became very successful and was used a lot by local businesses and the local community. That was the vehicle for getting the funding in, getting some good accommodation and for changing the ethos in the area so that the school was seen as a resource for education … There's still a lot you can do, whether it's at the business level or the community coming. So I'm trying to develop as much as I can that sense of purpose' (Headteacher).

Getting the context right will make ventures such as these much more likely to succeed.

Designing, re-designing and adapting the spaces

The more school leaders are aware of and respond positively to the expectations, needs and aspirations of those who are working in their community, the more they and their schools will reap the benefits. When it comes to teaching spaces, it is important to consider the needs and learning styles of all those who may be using them. According to Middlewood et al. (2005, p. 80):

> Schools can no longer be designed to deliver a restricted and heavily directed curriculum. They must have as a central objective the opportunity and flexibility to offer learning routes for a much wider potential market than just the 3–18 student population. They must become centres for learning and be flexible and imaginative resources accessed by all those who are interested in and excited by the possibility of extending their educational horizons.

They also need to be designed to cater for a wide variety of client users and a much broader range of activities. This can partly be achieved by people not being narrow-minded or territorial about teaching spaces: there is no reason for example why an art room during the day cannot be used for an adult literacy class in the evening. It can also be achieved by ensuring that new or re-furbished teaching areas are designed to be multi-use and as adaptable as possible.

A gut reaction to the challenge of having more people accessing the school for longer periods throughout the day would be to make the schools bigger. This is not necessarily the best solution as the following illustrates.

Case Example 9.1

Hugh Christie School is one of two secondary schools in the south-east of England trialling a government scheme that encourages schools to experiment with their use of time. The newly rebuilt college is smaller than its predecessor, despite having more students. In order to accommodate more users, they had to be much more flexible with time. By so doing, the school is open for much longer and start times have been staggered. Those students aged 15 or over begin at 10.30 a.m., two hours after the younger students. This still means that the school is at full stretch from 10.30 a.m. to 3.15 p.m., but it relieves pressure at either end of the day. There is less demand on laboratories, computer suites, sports facilities and specialist staff in the first and last parts of the day. It also means that the school is much more naturally inclined towards working longer hours with more flexible contracts for staff and greater opportunity for the local community to use the facilities. The principal has decided on this plan of action because he believes popular schools should expand but cannot be extended indefinitely without significant investment and space. In any case, he believes the answer is often not more buildings but better use of buildings.

Although we are now firmly in the twenty-first century, much of what is done when it comes to access to learning for students and other potential users is rooted in the nineteenth century. Paul Mortimer, a head who has been experimenting with school timetables for the last 20 years, points out that the traditional school year in the UK and elsewhere is modelled on factories where children of a similar age are split into management groups of 30. He adds:

> Students only spend about 15 per cent of their 38 weeks actually in school. The rest of the time is spent in eating, leisure or moving around. What we need to do is bite into that remaining 85 per cent of time while still sticking to the legal requirement of 38 teaching sessions a year.

We have visited innumerable schools, of all sizes and ages, where the ingenuity of leaders, governors, builders, and community helpers was evident in the conversion of traditional spaces – classrooms, kitchens, corridors, etc. – to modern, colourful, learner-friendly places. This had often been done at low cost and with local help, and the process itself had been a positive one for the school and a stimulus for the beginning of extended services. In Wellingborough, in the East Midlands of England, the clear commitment to Extended Services for the Christopher Hatton cluster began with a single room, re-designed, decorated, resourced and set aside for parents' use.

Many schools in the UK and elsewhere are already looking at radical strategies for delivering learning more effectively. While this may very well be good news for students of compulsory age (in that leaders and managers are now exploring ways in which to make *learning* more accessible rather than fitting *teaching* into pre-determined times and spaces), it is excellent news for the extended services initiative. The more flexible schools become, the more opportunity there is for all learners to take advantage of the available resources. And the more these resources are used, the more cost-effective they become. Many school leaders are thinking in terms of 24-hour schooling. Some ICT specialists are already talking of the 'intelligent school', where students will have round-the-clock access to a new kind of wireless network incorporating the internet, television and telephone through tiny devices in the fabric of their clothes. Virtual environments will allow learners to have lessons with other teachers in other schools or overseas. Although at the time of writing, such ideas might sound like science fiction, such is the pace of technological change that there is no reason why learning solutions like these will not be operational within the next decade. The implications for extended schools are clear: the ways in which schools are constructed and/or adapted now and in the future will need to have the following at their core:

- how best to utilize time and space for the benefit of all
- how to most effectively break with established procedures about how, when and where to deliver teaching and learning

- how to utilize and adapt existing so-called pedagogical truths imaginatively and strategically
- how to deploy and energize staff in quite different ways to make best use of their time and expertise.

Designing new spaces

Throughout the developed world, through the desire to update educational systems for economic competitiveness, thousands of new schools have been built. In the UK, for example, since the mid-1990s, well over £50 billion has been spent on building new schools or replacing old ones. At the outset, the emphasis was very much on addressing the chronic state of many of the country's schools and building flagship comprehensives and new 'academies', many of which were the brainchild of some of the world's most influential architects. The new designs were directed by the UK government's 'Building Schools for the Future' publication, which set down key principles about school design, not least the requirement that these schools moved away from traditional designs by creating more imaginative spaces, using high-tech, eco-friendly construction techniques and combining interior and exterior space much more imaginatively than had been the case in the past (see Middlewood et al., 2005, p. 6).

More recently, the impact of the Extended Services agenda has been exerting an increasing influence on school design, so that now the UK government is once again promoting guiding principles which will require schools to be designed and built to accommodate the requirements of the local and wider community much more prescriptively. Clear guidelines for further builds were set down in the UK by the government's education department to ensure that all schools develop extended facilities as part of any building programme.

Requirements included:

- making use of existing spaces outside the school day to run breakfast and after-school clubs
- providing childcare, adult learning, sporting and arts facilities after hours to local users
- remodelling or extending existing spaces to deliver additional services during the school day
- building major extensions or new buildings to deliver additional services such as Sure Start or nursery provision.

Central to these requirements was a determination to create facilities that could be used not only to deliver high-quality education for students but also to enrich the lives of their wider communities. Linked to this was the duty placed on architects, local authorities and school leaders to work cooperatively with their stakeholders and a range of partners and other service providers if they are to take maximum benefit from their new investment.

All this presents yet more challenges for school leaders. Designing or adapting a building for the twenty-first century which will respond sympathetically and imaginatively to the learning needs of children of compulsory school age is demanding enough. Creating flexible spaces for multi-agency use seven days a week (perhaps 24 hours a day!) is quite another thing. In order to make the right decisions, engage the right people and produce the best solution, certain fundamental strategies must be put in place. No list is comprehensive but we would consider the following considerations to be of crucial importance:

1. Employ well-qualified, tried and tested architects who know schools, understand what makes for effective teaching and learning spaces and who promote the Extended Services agenda. Ideally, they will have a detailed knowledge of the community in which the school will be operating. Insist on having them produce a master plan which will either drive the new design or direct the proposed new build/extension projects.
2. Audit clearly and extensively the potential stakeholders and users. These could include people who already work in the school, local, private and voluntary sector organizations, groups from further afield (who may up to this point have never been considered as potential users), local and regional business and charities. Assess closely what these users' needs are and accommodate them into the design process. Ensure that the needs of all the potential users are negotiated fairly and openly in a climate of mutual trust. As far as possible, give them what they want and be prepared to re-negotiate terms and conditions if this is what is needed to establish the partnership.
3. Consider how most effectively and seamlessly you can manage relationships between the daytime teaching staff and the staff or other agencies who may be using the same spaces for out-of-hours provision. Make sure that 'core business' staff are aware of the aims and purposes of FSES and how it can make a positive contribution to raising standards and improving practice.
4. Consider any and all of the risk assessment/health and safety implications of different users accessing the site at the same time. For example, running a crèche alongside vocational diplomas such as construction and engineering on the same site at the same time needs careful management in terms of location and access. Equally, issues such as appropriate car parking spaces, builders on-site, routine repair and maintenance programmes, etc. all have to be managed in the knowledge that multi-agency use of a site for much longer time spans needs to be very skilfully thought through.

5. Make sure, when the new spaces are being created, that practical considerations are incorporated into the design. For example:
  • are the reception areas appropriate?
  • is there sufficient security (including CCTV)?
  • are the toilets easily accessible and clearly signed?
  • are the disabled facilities up to standard?
  • does the alarm system allow for areas to be 'zoned out'?
  • is all the available interior and exterior space being utilized as efficiently and effectively as possible?

Obviously this list is not exhaustive and all schools are different: there is no single foolproof blueprint which will cater for all situations. The following example shows how well it can work when people cooperate and act together.

Case Example 9.2

The Campus, North Somerset, comprises a 420-place primary school, a nursery class, a 67-place special needs school for children with learning difficulties, a community learning and resource centre/library, sports hall, community/meeting rooms, Weston College facilities, a community police office, an outdoor sports and recreation space and a civic square. The project was born out of the needs of an emerging community in a new area of the UK's Weston-super-Mare. The innovative new building encourages access through the design. The front doors are on the pavement edge removing any boundaries between the building and the public. The community part of the building is the most open, with double-height glazing onto the street, and a reception desk to one side of the entrance to welcome visitors. It is an inviting, light and open space. The part of the building with the schools inside feels more solid and protective through the use of masonry, and is colour-coded to ease navigation. The building has areas that are shared between the schools and areas that are shared between the schools and the community. Broadly speaking, there is a community side and a schools side, insofar as they can be made completely separate. However, the design of the library and public areas encourages students to come in. The dining room and hall are shared facilities that can be accessed by everyone, and the servery is able to provide for both the school and the community areas. The playground is designed to encourage maximum integration with shared play spaces for the primary and special school pupils. Provision was made for greater segregation of the playground with low fences (including for the nursery pupils), but has hardly been needed. The playing fields are shared by all users of The Campus.

Finding the money!

School leaders committed to Extended Services can be permanently preoccupied with funding issues which, if allowed, will dominate much of their thinking. Much of what has been covered thus far in this chapter has real funding implications but the contributions of central governments are often inadequate. The lack of capital expenditure to help achieve the extended services agenda is perhaps difficult to fathom particularly when, as we have already said, the money spent in the UK on school buildings over the last 10 years has been far in excess of anything spent in the previous 100 years.

Entrepreneurial leaders will not, however be deterred by this. There is no magic formula to securing funding; any single success is more often than not achieved after several failures. Most headteachers who have established reputations for finding additional funding will say that it takes a great deal of time and effort, a lot of energy, a considerable amount of bare-faced cheek on occasion and more than a little luck. However, leaders of extended schools will still need to be dogged and methodical in their determination to track down any potential funding and apply for anything that looks as though it might produce a return. One major advantage of developing positive and formal links with other agencies – particularly from the charitable sector – does mean that many more funding streams are opened up. Joint applications are frequently more likely to be successful than those coming from a single institution.

Funding opportunities for extended services are not of course confined to the UK. Increasingly, grants are being made available to countries that might have been off the radar even 20 years ago. The work being done by the Charles Stewart Mott Foundation is a case in point.

Case Example 9.3

The (US) Charles Stewart Mott Foundation believes that learning how people can live together most effectively is one of the fundamental needs of humanity. In so doing, people create a sense of community, or belonging, whether at the local neighbourhood level or as a global society. The underpinning principle governing the Foundation's work is a commitment to the fact that building strong communities through collaboration provides a basis for positive change. They also consider that it is a requirement on their part to recognize strong and effective leadership and provide funding which will inspire the aspirations and potential of others. Since January 2007, five non-governmental organizations (NGOs) with extensive experience in developing and supporting community schools have received significant funds from the Foundation. Significantly, the partnerships receiving grants include

continued

> *continued*
>
> Russia where they are developing collaborations of students, parents, teachers and representatives from what are described as 'power circles', which include politicians, local government officials, businessmen and other influential members of the local community to bring about the required change. Other countries developing similar partnerships are the Ukraine, the Czech Republic and Moldova.

Those school leaders who are most successful at obtaining additional funding are invariably those who know, acknowledge and utilize the system. They capitalize quickly on any potential situations or opportunities as they arise and, according to Coleman (2006, p. 190), do not spend long hours analysing why applications have not been successful, primarily because they are busy working on the next!

> In addition to partnership working, maintaining an entrepreneurial approach is important in securing extra funds, and the school may need to develop additional complementary services. Such an entrepreneurial ethos is also important in promoting an openness to partnership activity and a willingness to engage in unexpected and opportunistic openings. (Coleman, ibid.)

Case Example 9.4

A secondary school in a deprived neighbourhood in outer London was attempting to find £100,000 to help it achieve specialist technology college status. An abbot at a nearby monastery approached the headteacher one day to ask if he would like to use (for free) a rarely used retreat house situated approximately two miles from the school for additional classroom/outreach work as they could no longer afford the upkeep of the building. The headteacher initially turned the offer down but on reflection went back to the abbot and asked if he was prepared to gift the building to them, in return for which the monastery would become the college's official technology college sponsors. He would then have the building valued on the open market and with luck raise the £100,000 he was seeking. The abbot eventually agreed. Ever the opportunist, this headteacher decided to take the matter one stage further. He knew the retreat house was surrounded by local housing and was therefore ripe for development. A local builder offered to buy it from him in order to knock it down and build much needed apartments for the neighbourhood. Instead of accepting cash for the property, he negotiated with the builder to erect (at cost) a much-needed three-storey technology block for his school. In the end, everyone benefited.

Although the above example is an extreme illustration of a school leader thinking on his feet and utilizing all the potential resources to best advantage, the basic principle of always being prepared to capitalize on situations to optimum effect is something all leaders of extended schools may need to note.

A theme running through this book has been the fact that leading an extended school does not mean that the leader has to be involved in every initiative. It is important (as we have said in Chapter 3) to practise distributed leadership and recognize that many of the areas of activity that an extended school will enter into require levels of expertise that school leaders may not have. This is equally true when it comes to accessing funding. Increasingly, school leaders are employing consultants who specialize in bid writing and seeking out any and all funding streams. They can be paid at an hourly rate or with a one-off management fee or have part of their fee linked to a percentage of any successful application. Whatever the arrangement, using experts in this way can be a much more cost-effective and efficient way of working than trying to do everything in-house.

Although there is always a measure of good fortune implicit in any successful acquisition of funds, headteachers can improve their chances of attracting additional capital by making sure they pursue strategies which are statistically more likely to bear fruit. They need to link potential funding streams carefully to their educational vision and the range of services their local community needs. They also have to consider the sustainability of services provided on their site including how they will be funded in the future. Furthermore, knowing why you need the money is crucial! Although in the UK, for example, much of the capital funding is not huge, it is nonetheless worth pursuing. The UK government has, for example, pledged £840 million from 2003–2008 specifically for schools to develop extended services. From 2008 onwards, schools will have £990 million through the personalization fund which can also, apparently, be used to support access to extended services, particularly for disadvantaged children. Remember too that the judicious use of funding can mean that not very much money can achieve a great deal – a point made by Dyson et al. (2002, p. 60):

> A relatively modest injection of funding stimulates a range of extended activities. This is because it tends to be combined with other forms of resourcing and may be used to leverage other funding into the school ... There is also good evidence that the combining of funding sources, legitimised by the dual use of facilities, generates more and better facilities than might otherwise be available to schools.

We encountered at least one cluster of schools offering very important and effective extended services across their community. The school leaders, when questioned about funding, told us they had relied solely so far on government funding and had done nothing about raising further funds. They admitted that when that central funding ceased, the services currently offered would no longer be tenable and 'We need to get round to doing something about tapping extra sources.' In that area, it would be tragic if the excellent initiatives begun by these leaders suddenly ceased because of a failure to think ahead about funding and sustainability. Indeed, the worst possible consequence would be a community backlash and loss of faith in the services.

In most developed countries, there are grants and charitable trusts which can be explored by school leaders as potential funding sources. For example, in England, in 2008, 'The Big Lottery Fund' invited bids of between £10,000 and £500,000 for its Family Learning programme. For smaller projects, 'Awards for All' offered between £300 and £10,000 for projects that enable people to take part in art, sport, heritage and community activities or that promote education, the environment and health in the local community. There are, as well, numerous charitable trusts and foundations that will fund projects. Similar funding mechanisms operate in other countries, and of course funding sources exist at international levels, e.g. European Community and United Nations funds.

Trying to get to grips with the often complex and time-consuming procedures for funding applications can be a task too far for some school leaders. However, there are ways of simplifying the process. Software packages such as Grantfinder can offer up-to-date and comprehensive information about all potential sources of funding. Many local authorities have departments that specialize in how to access external funding. There are other agencies such as local strategic partnerships that are set up to put funding providers in touch with organizations that most deserve financial support. Schools can also generate additional funding by capitalizing on the financial potential of their own site. Many schools have introduced a whole range of activities for which they charge – for example, childcare, after-school clubs and adult learning. In order to be profitable, fees have to be market-driven and cost-effective, as the following example illustrates.

Case Example 9.5

Delaware Community Primary School, on the Devon–Cornwall border, serves a diverse rural population, which includes pockets of real poverty, and charges £1.75 per session for all the activities it offers during out-of-school sessions. 'We asked how much people would be prepared to pay and started off charging £1.00, says headteacher Ms Grail. 'It's gone up year on year by 25p, and the numbers attending have also gone up, as the quality of what we're offering has improved. Parents can choose to pay upfront for a six-week block, or they can pay session by session.' Pam Geggie, the extended school coordinator, works 15 hours a week, collecting money, booking sessions and ensuring Criminal Records Bureau checks on staff have been made. Activities for the 200 pupils include chess, an art club,

continued

continued

gymnastics and drama, while those open to the local community range from the standard football and tag rugby (above) through cookery for teenagers to unicycle hockey and rock school. Delaware directly employs everyone who runs a session. All are paid the standard local sports coach rate of £12.00 an hour. 'It's tricky to get hold of people', admits Ms Grail. 'We grow our own – parents and teaching assistants are now training up.' Crucially, she says, 'We've responded to local needs and it's constantly evolving. When something hasn't worked, we've changed it. People come in numbers because they want what we're providing. Overall, it is self-financing.'

Although the sums of money being mentioned here are modest, applying such careful budgetary management can quite easily reap significant financial returns. In one sense, this example illustrates simply and effectively the fundamental truth about resources: making the most of what you have, trying out new and untried solutions to staffing and curriculum needs in order to deliver teaching and learning to a much broader clearly targeted clientele and accessing all and every funding opportunity are non-negotiable. Failure to deliver on these fronts will almost certainly mean that the objectives laid down by the extended services agenda will not be met.

Further reading

Coleman, M. and Anderson, L. (2000) *Managing Finance and Resources in Education.* London: Paul Chapman Publishing.

Keating, I. and Moorcroft, R. (2006) *Managing the Business of Schools*. London: Paul Chapman Publishing/Sage and NCSL.

Points to consider

- Remember that leading an extended school requires many of the qualities that go hand in hand with leading any successful organization – a point we make consistently throughout this book. However, when it comes to resources, leaders need to think in very different ways about how to find solutions to problems. It is not always about finding extra funding. Sometimes, utilizing existing resources in more radical ways can bring rewards. Are there current spaces, for example, that might be able to be converted into places that could offer a new facility?

- Employing skilled bid writers on a fixed fee or percentage basis is one easy method for improving your chances of success in gaining funds and reducing stress levels. Remember that, even if it often seems otherwise, there is a lot of funding available if you have the perseverance and single mindedness. If you do not use a bid writer at present, try detailing the time and money (and hassle) that writing a bid yourself involves.
- Do not be satisfied with anything in your school that militates against the organization coming across as professional and proactive. Other agencies do not wish to be associated with businesses that convey any sense of being sloppy or second-rate. How recently have you checked all your processes of communication with visitors (physical, written, spoken, etc.)?

10
Conclusions

Over the last two years, we have spent a great deal of time investigating in depth the extent to which this initiative will impact on learning in its widest, most accessible sense. Our initial excitement about the potential this innovation has to bring about radical change in the way education operates has, if anything, increased. This is because our many visits to schools and our discussions with leaders at all levels – headteachers, extended schools coordinators, parents, stakeholders, agency workers, support services – have revealed a huge enthusiasm for and firm commitment to extended schools in all their forms. Nobody has said that moving this agenda on is straightforward, but almost everyone we have talked to has been convinced that the obstacles can be overcome, that the potential for positive change is immense and that the efforts are and will be absolutely worthwhile.

Leaders and managers of extended schools: some lessons learnt

The following points came through very strongly from the leaders and managers we met:

- Without an unswerving commitment to the fundamental philosophy underpinning extended schooling, no real or significant progress is going to be made. This commitment needs to be centred on a belief that this is not simply that *Every Child Matters* but that *Everybody Matters*. This applies to whatever community context a school is operating in. As we noted early on in the book, leaders of extended schools will be clear that everyone, regardless of class, social background and/or economic well-being, has a need and a right to access lifelong learning.
- Schools cannot do this on their own! Unless leaders attempt to engage all rele-

vant stakeholders, both within their respective organizations and in the local and wider community, they will not be able to establish the range of partnerships required to deliver what is needed.

- All leaders involved in extended schools need to be both radical and methodical. By being radical, they will look to move away from safe, established practice. There is no way, as the many examples in this book illustrate, that making learning accessible to a much wider target audience for much longer periods will happen if leaders are not prepared, on many occasions, to throw away the rule book. However, equally important is the need to be measured, highly-organized and methodical in laying down secure foundations for these radical solutions.

This will take time!

One conclusion from our research is an important message for school leaders setting out on the path of extended schooling with a commitment to a vision of making a real difference to their communities – it is a long process. Making an early impact is important, but in most cases the real changes necessary may take a very long time. More than one leader already well down the path recognized that the transformation would occur gradually and well beyond their own career contribution. One anecdote from a long-serving senior learning mentor, well qualified and thoroughly practical, made the point for us very powerfully. We believe this is worth sharing:

Pamela told how she had visited deprived families in their homes in Nottingham in the 1990s. She recalled one visit to a disorganized household with a young mother and several young children, including a toddler ('Karen') sitting on the floor, 'wet and noisily bawling'. The mother ignored the toddler apart from yelling at her occasionally and threatening to 'belt you one'. Pamela had picked the child up and tried gently to explain that she needed changing and pacifying if possible. The mother responded but said she usually didn't 'have time for all that'.

Fifteen years later, Pamela is running groups for 'young mums' in the Centre, part of the school complex, and is explaining to one of the mothers, aged 17, about how parenting involves patience and trying to 'bond' with the baby. Hearing the mother's name is Karen, she checks the surname, and realizes this mother is the wet, noisy toddler from all those years ago, repeating the pattern of teenage pregnancy and parenthood at 16. Karen, however, in feedback on the groups says, 'I know now that hitting my baby and shouting at it doesn't do much good. I try all kinds of other things and feel I know what being a mum really means. I think I *can be a good mum.*' A year later, Karen is training to be one of the helpers in the groups, gaining accreditation to eventually be a group leader for other young mothers! In other words, a whole generation passed but Pamela and her colleagues drew inspiration from this small example that attitudes can change. The Karens of this world do want to learn and Karen's own children have every chance of a much improved upbringing, learning and life.

This understanding by extended school leaders of the time span needed for community change fits with the new concept of educational leadership as having a responsibility way beyond a single organization. Some educationalists see this form as 'system leadership'; Hopkins (2007, p. 153), for example, calls these system leaders headteachers who 'care about and work for the success of other schools as well as their own'. Those leaders we spoke to do not care for the term 'system leadership', seeing it as too impersonal and lacking specific ethical purpose. As 'community leaders', their preferred term, they saw their role as 'creating a shared belief in possibilities' (Riley et al., 2007, p. 39).

So what are the major challenges?

A clear message that has come through from our research is that there are many challenges, risks, disappointments and problems that will have to be faced. The following, however, have emerged as being of particular importance:

- Leaders have to be able to build and sustain capacity. For example, more than one cluster is concerned that even with secure funding, the capacity in their local communities to resource growing demand may be limited. The Hatton Partnership in Wellingborough, Northamptonshire, is facing huge demands for provision for those new residents for whom English is a second language. While demand is just being met at present, the growing immigrant population means it will continue to increase. The training requirements for tutors are considerable and there is a worry about not being able to meet this demand. This level of concern about how to find ways of meeting current and future demand was echoed by several community partnerships we visited. It is clearly a major issue, especially for those which are fast-growing and evolving.
- There will be an ongoing challenge (some might say battle!) to find the necessary levels of funding and capital investment to enable leaders to deliver the extended services agenda. There are major implications in terms of school buildings, staffing practices and routine maintenance and provision that are not in any sense being addressed by central government(s). The need to be relentless and professional in securing these additional resources is a fundamental prerequisite for success.
- Succession planning at educational leadership level has emerged as a significant issue in virtually all developed countries. All the evidence to date shows that fewer and fewer applicants of real quality and experience are prepared to take on the responsibilities of leadership at the highest level. This situation is potentially exacerbated by the emergence of the extended services agenda. Not only will schools be looking to appoint so-called conventional leaders, they will also need

to recruit people who have the ability, drive and determination to make extended services work. In addition, they will need to have procedures in place to ensure that the people following them are equally skilled and committed!

• As crucial as everything already mentioned is the need to establish, nurture and develop the right partnerships for the right reason at the right time – a point we have stressed on several occasions in the book. For this to happen, school leaders will need to be in tune with how their communities work and what their needs are. They have to be aware of how these other agencies/stakeholders can be brought effectively and purposefully into working partnerships for the benefit of all those involved. They also need to be brave and perceptive enough to acknowledge when these partnerships have ceased to be productive. It can require skill, diplomacy, organization, patience and negotiation of the highest order if real collaboration and partnership networking are going to succeed.

The differences between ECM in the UK and NCLB in the USA

We have referred to the apparently parallel initiatives in the USA and the UK, so how do the prospects of success for ECM in the UK look, compared with NCLB in the USA?

The two programmes, each enshrined in specific legislation, although similarly named, have significant differences in their intentions and approaches. Both set out to reduce inequalities in educational provision and to raise achievement levels for those seen as disadvantaged. However, according to some powerful critiques of NCLB, such as those of Darling-Hammond (2007), it has actually left many of the children it was supposed to help worse off through an obsession with measuring achievement by test scores, leading to a narrowing of teaching focus, as schools become fearful of being seen as failing and thereby losing resources. The solutions proposed by critics relate to the supply, deployment and retention of high-quality teachers.

While these would improve educational attainment, it is doubtful whether such solutions can deal with the underlying causes of underachievement of many children. Darling-Hammond (2007) refers to 'poverty linked to poor pre-natal and childhood health care, low birth weight, poor nutrition, lead poisoning, maternal substance abuse ...' as examples of issues which remain untouched in most areas by the implementation of NCLB.

ECM, on the other hand, attempts to tackle some of the same issues of underachievement and unequal provision through a focus on integrating educational provision with the provision for improved health service support, childcare support and social welfare. It does this by 'extending' this integrated support from birth or very early years through until at least early adulthood, and encouraging the links with adult learning and learning for life. Although at the time of writing, there are many areas still relatively untouched by this extension initiative, the signs are that where it is applied, it can work by affecting the quality of life led by community members, channelled through the educational provision for each individual child.

While we have seen many excellent examples of extended schools and indeed of the beginnings of community transformation, we are realistic enough to know that these do not and will not represent an accurate universal picture. We do feel, through our research and through feedback from many involved in this field, that there are reasons why this particular 'community initiative' may succeed.

- Unlike several previous community education initiatives in the UK, extended schooling has the full support of central government, and not merely regional bodies. While support from the centre can and may wax and wane over the years, the impetus is far greater than ever before.
- This initiative is inseparably linked with initiatives that are not simply education-focused. Through ECM and The Children's Act, extended schools have the power to make an impact on all the different facets of a child's development, especially the family. As Allen (2008, p. 7) puts it, this is 'evolutional in that we have ceased treating a child's difficulties in isolation'. The central commitment to integrated services underlines this positive view of extended schooling (Woolmer, 2008).
- In the best extended school practice, the services needed locally are being identified by the communities themselves and not by some external, supposedly 'wise' authority, whether that be national government, regional government or indeed the local school. Solutions therefore are much more likely to be owned and implemented by those communities.
- There is a huge commitment to early intervention and prevention, rather than remedial or aftercare. Surely, in the long term, this *is* the only way ahead. Levin and Fullan (2008, p. 301) argue that it is now clear that genuine change or 'system renewal' has to 'include deep attention (finally) to early childhood capacity-building from conception to age five, the well-being of students of all ages, and adult education, particularly as a complement to the development of young children'.
- Much of the best practice we have seen is building in sustainability from the start of the enterprise, capitalizing on the far greater awareness that there is today of sustainability in the modern context.
- There is early evidence (Cummings et al., 2007) that there have already been positive outcomes for poorer families, and that the achievement gap between advantaged and disadvantaged pupils is narrower in extended schools than in others.

Although there are concerns about succession planning (above), we believe that national governments are now much more focused on addressing and solving this vital issue. Therefore, another positive is that as new headteachers and principals come through from middle-leadership roles, more will be imbued with ECM and the commitments it carries. The training of leaders will adjust more and more in this way and 'the possibility exists that leadership development programmes may emphasise the social justice agenda as never before' (Brundrett and Anderson de Cuevas, 2007, p. 47).

The future?

Theories and ideas about leadership including educational leadership continue to abound and Rayner (2008, p. 44) believes that modern inclusive leadership involves 'reciprocal purposeful learning in a community'. This description seems to us to embody much of what extended school leaders are illustrating in their work. As the initiative evolves, so will the leaders and their leadership. Most significantly, it would seem to us, the fundamental characteristics of this initiative – for example, risk-taking, radical thinking, entrepreneurialism, dogged determination, passion for learning, belief in dynamic partnerships – mirror those qualities which are most often to be found in effective leaders.

The understanding that extended schools are 'not just breakfast clubs' but are about ultimate community transformation and greater social justice is what we have found to be the key to successful leadership and management of extended schools. At the heart of this understanding is the belief that every child matters and no child should be left behind. There is no doubt, in our view, that future genera-tions will look back in incredulity that any of their predecessors could or would have contemplated managing teaching and learning in any other way.

Further reading

Glover, D. and Harris, A. (2007) *'Every Child Matters' and 'Extended Schools': A Review of the Literature*. Coventry: University of Warwick.

References

Allen, T. (2008) 'Wraparound for Success for Wychall', *Extended Schools Update*, 4: 7–9. London: Optimus Professional Publishing.

Anderson, L. (2000) 'The Move to Entrepreneuralism', in M. Coleman and L. Anderson (eds) *Managing Finance and Resources in Education*. London: Paul Chapman Publishing.

Apps, J., Reynolds, J., Ashby, V. and Husain, F. (2007) *Family Support in Children's Centres*. London: The Family and Parenting Institute.

Ball, S. (1999) 'Labour, Learning and the Economy: A "policy sociology perspective"'. *Cambridge Journal of Education*, 29(2): 195–206.

Barton, C. (2008) 'Parents of Teenagers Support Group', *Extended Schools Update*, 2: 4–6. London: Optimus Publishing.

Bastiani, J. (1987) *Perspectives on Home–School Relations*. Slough: NFER-Nelson.

Bell, L. (1999) 'Back to the Future', *Journal of Educational Administration*, 37(3): 205–16.

Bond, K. and Farrar, M. (2005) *Leaders and Partners: Networking in the Wider Community*. Nottingham: NCSL.

Bottery, M. (2004) *The Challenges of Educational Leadership*. London: Paul Chapman Publishing.

Bradbury, R. (2007) 'Thinking Aloud', *School Financial Management*, 89: 6. London: Optimus Professional Publishing.

Brown, K. and White, K. (2006) *Exploring the Evidence Base for Integrated Children's Services*. Edinburgh: Scottish Executive Education Department.

Brown, P. (1997) 'Education and the Idea of Parentocracy', in A. Halsey, H. Lauder, P. Brown and A. Wells (eds) *Education: Culture, Economy, Society*. Oxford: Oxford University Press.

Brundrett, M. and Anderson de Cuevas, R. (2007) 'Setting an Agenda for Social Justice through Leadership Development', *Management in Education*, 21(4): 44–8.

Bull, T. (1989) 'Home–School Links: Family-oriented or business-oriented?', *Educational Review*, 41(2): 113–19.

Bush, T. (2008) *Leadership and Management Development in Education*. London: Paul Chapman Publishing.

Bush, T. and Middlewood, D. (2005) *Leading and Managing People in Education*. London: Paul Chapman Publishing.

Carpenter, B. (2005) 'Real Prospects for Early Childhood Intervention'. in B. Carpenter and J. Egerton (eds) *Early Childhood Intervention*. Coventry: West Midlands SEN Regional Partnership.

Carpenter, B. (2008) 'Emotional Health in Children', speech to SSAT Primary School Conference, Birmingham, March.

Clayton, T. (1993) 'From Domestic Helper to Assistant Teacher: the changing role of the classroom assistant', *European Journal of Special Needs Education*, 8(1): 32–44.

Clough, P. and Corbett, J. (2000) *Theories of Inclusive Education*. London: Paul Chapman Publishing.

Coleman, A. (2006a) *Collaborative Leadership in Extended Schools*. Nottingham: National College for School Leadership.

Coleman, A. (2006b) *Lessons from Extended Schools*. Nottingham: National College for School Leadership.

Comenius Project (2003) *Best Practice Guide to Improve the Relationship between Home and School*. Coventry: ContinYou.

Cousins, S. (2005) 'Curriculum Reform in Northern Ireland', in J. West-Burnham and M. Coates (eds) *Personalising Learning*. Stafford: Network Educational Press.

Crossley, D. (2002) 'From Factory School to Modern Working and Learning Environment', *Headship Matters*, 15: 3–4. London: Optimus Professional Publishing.

Crossley, D. (2003) 'From factory school to virtual school,' *Headship Matters*, 16: 3–4. London: Optimus Professional Publishing.

Crozier, G. (2000) *Parents and Schools: Partners or protagonists?* Stoke-on-Trent: Trentham Books.

Cummings, C. (2008) 'An Important Part of the Jigsaw', *Extended Schools Update*, 4: 2. London: Optimus Professional Publishing.

Cummings, C., Dyson, A. and Todd, L. (2005) *Evaluation of the Full-Service Extended Schools Project: End of First Year Report*. London: DfES.

Cummings, C., Dyson, A., Mujis, D., Papps, I., Raffo, C., Tiplady, L. and Todd, L. with Crowther, D. (2007) *Evaluation of the Full-Service Schools Initiative: Final Report*, available at http/www.dfes.govukresearch/data/uploadfiles/RR852.pdf/

Darling-Hammond, L.(2007) 'Race, Inequality and Educational Accountability: The irony of No Child Left Behind', *Race, Ethnicity and Education*, 10(3): 245–60.

Davies, B. (2005) 'The Essentials of School Leadership', in B. Davies (ed.) *The Essentials of School Leadership*. London: Paul Chapman Publishing.

Desforges, C. with Abonchaat, A. (2003) *The Impact of Parental Involvement, Parental Support and Family Education on Pupil Achievement and Adjustment: A literature review*. London, DfES.

DfE (1994) *Schools and Careers Education*. London: HMSO.

DfES (2002) *Schools for the Future: Designing Learning Communities*. London: DfES.

DfES (2004) *Every Child Matters*. London: DfES.

DfES (2005a) *Extended Schools: Access to Opportunities and Services for All*. London: DfES.

DfES (2005b) 'Youth Matters – What Next?' Nottingham: DfES Publications.

DfES (2006a) *Multi Agency Working: Introduction and Overview*. London: DfES.

DfES (2006b) *Planning and Funding Extended Schools*. Nottingham: DfES Publications.

DfES/PricewaterhouseCoopers (2007) *Independent Study into School Leadership*. London: DfES.

Dimmock, C. (2000) *Designing the Learner-centred School*. London: Falmer Press.

Draper, I. (2000) 'From Appraisal to Performance Management', *Professional Development Today*, 3(2): 11–21.

Dryfoos, J., Quinn, J. and Barkin, C. (2005) *Community Schools in Action*. Oxford: Oxford University Press.

Dyson, A. (2006) 'What are we Learning from Research?', in J. Piper (ed.) *Schools Plus to Extended Schools*. Coventry: ContinYou.

Dyson, A., Millward, A. and Todd, L. (2002) 'A Study of Extended Schools Demonstration Projects', Research Report 381, London: DfES.

Foskett, N. and Lumby, J. (2003) *Leading and Managing Education: International Dimensions*. London: Paul Chapman Publishing.

Frean, A. (2007) 'Children who go to Nursery Full-time Become Anti-social', *Times*, April, p. 9.

Frederick, K. (2006) 'Heads and Teachers don't Have to Do it all', *Times Educational Supplement*, May.

Frost, N. (2005) 'Professionalism, Partnership and Joined-up Thinking', *Research in Practice*, Dartington: Dartington Hall Trust.

Fullan, M. (1998) 'Leadership for the Twenty-first Century: Breaking the bonds of dependency', *Educational Leadership*, 55(7): 6–10.

Gelsthorpe, A. (2006) 'Extended Schools – The story so far', in J. Piper (ed.) *Schools Plus to Extended Schools*. Coventry: ContinYou.

Glatter, R. (2002) 'Governance, Autonomy and Accountability in Education', in T. Bush and L. Bell (eds) *Principles and Practice of Educational Management*. London: Sage Publications.

Gleeson, D. and Husbands, C. (2001) *The Performing School*. London: Routledge-Falmer.

Glover, D. and Harris, A. (2007) *'Every Child Matters' and 'Extended Schools': A Review of the Literature*. Coventry: University of Warwick.

Guardian Education (2008) 'Parental support makes the difference', 19 February, pp. 6–7.

Harber, C. (1989) *Politics in African Education*. London: MacMillan.

Hargreaves, A. (1997) 'Restructuring Restructuring: Postmodernity and the prospects for educational change', in A. Halsey, H. Lauder, P. Brown and A. Wells (eds) *Education: Culture, Economy, Society*. Oxford: Oxford University Press.

Harker, M. (2001) 'How to Build Solutions at Meetings', in A. Amjal and I. Rees (eds) *Solutions in Schools*. London: Brief Therapy Press.

Harris, A. and Spillane, J. (2008) 'Distributed leadership through the looking glass', *Management in Education*, 22(1): 31–4.

Hentschke, G. and Caldwell, B. (2007) 'Entrepreneurial Leadership', in B. Davies (ed.) *The Essentials of School Leadership*. London: Paul Chapman Publishing.

Hill, R. (2008) *Achieving More Together and Adding Value through Partnerships*. London: Esmee Fairbairn Foundation.

Hopkins, D. (2007) *Every School a Great School*. Maidenhead: Open University Press/McGraw-Hill.

Hussein, N. (2008) 'Meeting the Community's Needs', *Extended Schools Update*, 3: 7–9. London: Optimus Professional Publishing.

Kaderoglou, E. and Drossinou, M. (2005) 'Early Intervention Services in Greece: Present situation and future prospects', in M. Guralnick (ed.) *The Developmental Systems Approach to Early Intervention*. Baltimore, MD: Paul H. Brookes.

Kam, H. and Gopinathan, S. (1999) 'Recent Developments in Singapore', *School Effectiveness and Improvement*, 10(1): 99–118.

Kelly, A. (1987) *Knowledge and Curriculum Planning*. London: Harper & Row.

Kendall, S., Lamont, E., Wilkin, A. and Kinder, K. (2007) *Every Child Matters: How School Leaders in Extended Schools Respond to Local Needs*. Slough: NFER.

Kerry, C. and Kerry, T. (2003) 'Policy and the Effective Employment and Deployment of Support Staff in Schools', *International Studies in Educational Administration*, 31(1): 65–81.

Kotter, J. (1995) 'Leading Change: Why transformation efforts fail', *Harvard Business Review*, 73: 22–5.

Lanners, R. and Mombaerts, D. (2000) 'Evaluation of Parents' Satisfaction with Early Intervention Services within and among European Countries', *Infants and Young Children*, 12(3): 61–70.

Leadbeater, C. (2005) *The Shape of Things to Come*. Nottingham: DfES Publications.

Leithwood, K. (2001) 'Criteria for Appraising School Leaders in an Accountable Policy Context', in D. Middlewood and C. Cardno (eds) *Managing Teacher Appraisal and Performance: An international perspective*. London: RoutledgeFalmer.

Levin, B. and Fullan, M. (2008) 'Learning about System Renewal', *Educational Management Administration and Leadership*, 36(2): 289–303.

Levine, J. (2005) 'Anxiety and Depression among Adolescents', Report for Washington, DC Schools Education Project.

Lewin, H. and Kelley, C. (1997) 'Can Education do it Alone?', in A. Halsey, H. Lauder, P. Brown and A. Wells (eds) *Education: Culture, Economy, Society*, Oxford: Oxford University Press.

Linley, R. (2008) 'A collaborative Approach to Student and Family Support', *Extended Schools Update*, 1: 4–6. London: Optimus Professional Publishing.

Lockyer, A. (2003) 'The Political Status of Children and Young People', in A. Lockyer, B. Crick and J. Annette (eds) *Education for Democratic Citizenship*. Aldershot: Aldgate Press.

Longenecker, G. and Ludwig, D. (1995) 'Ethical dilemmas in performance appraisal revisited', in J. Holloway, J. Lewis and G. Molloy (eds) *Performance Measurement and Evaluation*. London: Sage.

MacBeath, J., Gray, J., Cullen, J., Frost, D., Steward, S. and Swaffield, S. (2007) *Schools on the Edge*. London: Paul Chapman Publishing.

Maynard, C. (2007) 'Made for Each Other', *Schools ETC*, 4: 18–19.

Mayo, M. (2003) in L. Tett 'Working in Partnership', *NIACE Lifelines in Adult Learning*, No. 9. Nottingham: National Institute for Adult Continuing Education.

Mendez, H. (2005) 'Parent Involvement and Leadership in Action', in J. Dryfoos, J. Quinn and C. Barkin (eds) *Community Schools in Action*. Oxford: Oxford University Press.

Middlewood, D. (1997) 'Managing Staff Development', in T. Bush and D. Middlewood (eds) *Managing People in Education*. London: Paul Chapman Publishing.

Middlewood, D. (1999) 'Managing Relationships between Schools and Parents', in J. Lumby and N. Foskett (eds) *Managing External Relations in Schools and Colleges*. London: Paul Chapman Publishing.

Middlewood, D. (2001) 'The Future of Teacher Performance and Appraisal', in D. Middlewood and C. Cardno (eds) *Teacher Appraisal and Performance: An international perspective*. London: RoutledgeFalmer.

Middlewood, D. (2004) *Report on the Inclusion Mark in a Group of Leicester Schools*. Leicester: Ellesmere College/Leading Edge.

Middlewood, D. and Cardno, C. (2001) *Managing Teacher Appraisal and Performance: A Comparative Approach*. London: RoutledgeFalmer.

Middlewood, D. and Parker, R. (2001) 'Managing Curriculum Support Staff', in D. Middlewood and N. Burton (eds) *Managing the Curriculum*. London: Paul Chapman Publishing.

Middlewood, D., Parker, R. and Beere, J. (2005) *Creating a Learning School*. London: Paul Chapman Publishing/Sage.

Mitchell, B. (2005) *Extended Service Schools/ Inclusive Learning and Health Centres*. Leicester: Beauchamp College.

Mortimore, P. (1997) 'Can Effective Schools Compensate for Society?', in A. Halsey, H. Lauder, P. Brown and A. Wells (eds) *Education: Culture, Economy, Society*. Oxford: Oxford University Press.

Ng, S-W. (1999) 'Home–School Relations in Hong Kong: Separation or partnership', *School Effectiveness and Improvement*, 9(4): 473–90.

Nolan, A. (1996) *Spending Public Money: Governance and Audit Issues*. London: HMSO.

O'Neill, J. (1997) 'Teach, Learn, Appraise: The impossible triangle', in J. O'Neill (ed.) *Teacher Appraisal in New Zealand*. Palmerston: ERDC Press.

O'Neill, O. (2006) Speech at launch of Cambridge Assessment Network, Cambridge.

OECD (1997) *Parents as Partners in Schooling*. Paris: OECD.

Ofsted (2003) *Leadership and Management: Managing the School Workforce*. London: HMI.

Ofsted (2006) *Extended Services in Schools and Children's Centres*. HMI 2609. London: Ofsted.

Ofsted (2008) *How Well are they Doing? The Impact of Children's Centres and Extended Schools*. London: Ofsted.

Paton, R. and Vangen, S. (2004) *Understanding and Developing Leadership in Multi-Agency Children and Family Teams*. London: DfES.

Piper, J. (2003) 'Extended Schools: The dream of the future?', in T. Gelsthorpe and

J. West-Burnham (eds) *School and Community Leadership*. Harlow: Pearson.

Piper, J. (2006) *Schools Plus to Extended Schools: Lessons from the Last Five Years*. Coventry: ContinYou.

Popple, K. (1995) *Analysing Community Work: Its Theory and Practice*. Buckingham: Open University Press.

Power, M. (1996) *The Audit Explosion*. London: Demos.

Pugh, G. (1989) 'Parents and Professionals in Pre-school Services: Is partnership possible?', in S. Wolfendale (ed.) *Parental Involvement: Developing networks between home, school and community*. London: Cassell.

Rayner, S. (2008) 'Complexity, Diversity and Management: Some reflections on folklore and learning leadership in education', *Management in Education*, 22(2): 40–6.

Restemeuer, R. (2008) *The Children's Society: Annual Report*. London: Children's Society.

Riley, K. with Edge, K., Jordan, J. and Reed, J. (2007) *Thriving and Surviving as an Urban Leader: Reflective and analytical tools for leaders of our city schools*. London: Esmee Fairbairn Foundation and London Centre for Leadership in Learning, Institute of Education.

Robinson, V. and Timperley, H. (1996) 'Learning to be Responsive: The impact of school choice and decentralisation', *Educational Management and Administration*, 24(1): 65–78.

Rogers, P. (2008) 'A day in the life of ...', *Extended Schools Update*, 1: 10–11. London: Optimus Professional Publishing.

Rudd, P., Lines, A., Sohegen, S., Smith, R. and Reakes, A. (2003) 'Partnership Approaches to Sharing Best Practice', LEA Research Report 54. Slough: NFER.

Sammons, P., Power, S., Elliot, K., Robertson, P., Campbell, C. and Whitty, G. (2003) *New Community Schools in Scotland – Final Report – National Evaluation*. London: Institute of Education, University of London.

Schools ETC (2007) 'The Ties That Bind', Issue 7, December.

Scott, D. (1999) 'Accountability in education systems: centralising and decentralising pressures,' in J. Lumby and N. Foskett (eds) *Managing External Relations in Schools and Colleges*. London: Paul Chapman Publishing.

Sergiovanni, T. (1996) *Leadership for the Schoolhouse*. San Francisco, CA: Jossey-Bass.

Sikes, P.(1997) *Parents who Teach*. London: Cassell.

Singapore Teachers Union (STU) (2000) *Towards a World Class Education System through Enlightened School Management/Leadership and Meaningful Educational Activities*. Singapore: STU.

Smith, R. (2006) 'Strategies to ensure every child matters in your school', *Primary Headship*, 28: 8–9. London: Optimus Professional Publishing.

Snowden, M. (2004) 'Every Child Matters: The Contribution of Family Learning', A scoping paper. Nottingham: National Institute For Adult Continuing Education.

Snowden, M. (2006) 'Sustaining Partnerships', NIACE policy discussion paper. Nottingham: National Institute for Adult Continuing Education.

Stevens, J. (2007) 'Engaging Parents', *Schools ETC*, 6: 12. Coventry: ContinYou.

Strike, K. (2000) 'Community Coherence and Inclusiveness', Paper presented at 5th Annual Values and Educational Leadership Conference, Barbados, September.

Sylva, K., Melhuish, E., Sammons, P., Siraj-Blatchford, I. and Taggart, B. (2004) 'The effective provision of Pre-school Education Project: Technical Paper 12 – The Final Report: Effective Pre-school Education', London: DES/Institute of Education, University of London.

Tett, L. (2003) 'Working in Partnership', *NIACE Lifelines in Adult Learning, No. 9.* Nottingham: National Institute for Adult Continuing Education.

Timperley, H. and Robinson, V. (1998) 'The micropolitics of accountability,' *Educational Policy*, 12(2): 162–76.

Todd, L. (2007) *Partnerships for Inclusive Education.* London: Routledge.

Training and Development Agency (TDA) (2007) *Staffing and Workload.* London: TDA.

Troedson, H. (2005) *Mental Health: A Report for the World Health Organization.* Geneva and London: WHO.

UNICEF (2007) *Child Poverty in Perspective.* Geneva and London: UNICEF.

West-Burnham, J. (2005) 'Understanding Personalisation', in J. West-Burnham and M. Coates (eds) *Personalising Learning.* Stafford: Network Educational Press.

West-Burnham, J. (2006) 'Extended Schools in 2020: Prospects and possibilities', in J. Piper (ed.) (2006) *Schools Plus to Extended Schools: Lessons from the Last Five Years.*

Whalley, M. (1994) *Learning to be Strong: Setting up a neighbourhood service for under fives and their families.* London: Hodder and Stoughton.

Wilkins, R. (2005) 'Is Schooling a Technology, a Process of Socialisation, or a Consumer Product?', *Management in Education*, 19(1): 25–31.

Williams, P. (2002) 'The Competent Boundary Spanner', *Public Administrations*, 8(1). Oxford: Blackwell Synergy.

Wilson, N. (2008) 'Bringing Social Work into School', *Extended Schools Update*, 5: 7–9. London: Optimus Professional Publishing.

Wilson,V., Schlapp, U. and Davidson, J. (2003) 'An Extra Pair of Hands', *Educational Management and Administration*, 31(2): 189–205.

Wolfendale, S. (1996) 'The Contribution of Parents to Children's Achievements in School', in J. Bastiani and S. Wolfendale (eds) *Home–School Work in Britain.* London: David Fulton.

Woodland, J. (2007) 'Approaching Extended Schooling.' Presentation to seminar, Oadby, Leicester.

Woods, P. (2005) *Democratic Leadership in Education.* London: Paul Chapman Publishing.

Woolmer, P. (2008) 'Community Use: An old idea whose day has finally come?', *Extended Schools Update*, 4: 3. London: Optimus Professional Publishing.

Index

Added to a page number 'f' denotes a figure and 't' denotes a table.